An Attitude and Approach for Teaching Music to Special Learners

SECOND EDITION

Elise S. Sobol

Published in partnership with
MENC: The National Association for Music Education
Frances S. Ponick, Executive Editor

Rowman & Littlefield Education
Lanham • New York • Toronto • Plymouth, UK

Published in partnership with
MENC: The National Association for Music Education

Published in the United States of America
by Rowman & Littlefield Education
A Division of Rowman & Littlefield Publishers, Inc.
A wholly owned subsidary of The Rowman & Littlefield Publishing Group, Inc.
4501 Forbes Boulevard, Suite 200, Lanham, Maryland 20706
www.rowmaneducation.com

Estover Road
Plymouth PL6 7PY
United Kingdom

British Library Cataloguing in Publication Information Available

Library of Congress Cataloging-in-Publication Data

Sobol, Elise S.
    An attitude and approach for teaching music to special learners /
Elise S. Sobol.—2nd ed.
        p. cm.
    "Published in partnership with MENC, The National Association for Music
Education."
    Includes bibliographical references and index.
    ISBN-13: 978-1-57886-856-8 (pbk. : alk. paper)
    ISBN-10: 1-57886-856-4 (pbk. : alk. paper)
    eISBN-13: 978-1-57886-913-8
    eISBN-10: 1-57886-913-7
    1. Music—Instruction and study. 2. Special education. 3. Children with
disabilities—Education. I. Title.
MT17.S63 2008
371.9'04487—dc22   2008021724

™
 The paper used in this publication meets the minimum requirements
of American National Standard for Information.Sciences—Permanence of
Paper for Printed Library Materials, ANSI/NISO Z39.48-1992.
Manufactured in the United States of America.

Table of Contents

Foreword

WITH FEDERAL special education laws more than thirty years old, it is still difficult to find practical strategies to apply in our classrooms. It is even more difficult to find materials that resonate from a paradigm rooted in genuine care and concern for students.

Educating students in a truly inclusive environment includes nurturing a shift in attitudes toward students with disabilities, as well as toward those simply noted as "different." In this book, Elise Sobol brings to the table a set of classroom-tested strategies and techniques designed to respect the personhood of every child.

Sobol is genuinely excited about sharing her classroom experiences with other music educators. She reminds us of the joy in celebrating individual student improvement and the successes of all teachers and students. Furthermore, she shares these not only from her years of experience, but also from her heart.

Occupying a place in my office, this book reminds me of the importance of considering each individual student when preparing instruction. This second edition introduced me to mediated learning experiences and how they can be used with special learners. Moreover, having this book at hand keeps me connected to Elise Sobol's unbridled excitement and hopeful optimism about the potential of even those most greatly affected by their disabilities. Her sincere belief that *all* students possess innate musical ability that can be nurtured in the classroom is refreshing and inspiring.

Alice M. Hammel, DMA
graduate faculty,
James Madison and Christopher Newport Universities
special learners chair, Virginia Music Educators Association

Preface

THE YEARS of experience teaching as an early childhood, regular, and special education music teacher; college professor; and guest speaker, both here and abroad, have taught me that teaching is so much more than a profession. Teaching is a commitment to the belief that each child is unique and completely whole, no matter what challenges the child faces. Teaching is a commitment to the belief that each child is here to make a contribution with his or her life and that through music, children can communicate and gain skills for academic achievement and social, emotional, and psychological well-being. My attitude and approach for teaching music to special learners include the following seven foundations: a teacher's love of children, understanding those with special needs, training, skill, presentation of materials through a reality-based system that uses multisensory techniques, active patience, and the belief in the positive and the possible. *An Attitude and Approach for Teaching Music to Special Learners* was developed in large part since 1993 through my service work as the New York State School Music Association chairperson for special learners. It is intended to be a resource for the mind and spirit—a handbook to bring a joy of music and life success to students of all ages and learning styles.

Acknowledgments

A S I ACKNOWLEDGED in the 2001 first edition, my sincere thanks go to the hundreds and hundreds of special children whom I have had the pleasure of teaching. They have blessed me with their winning spirit and in so doing have lit the way for my attitude and approach for teaching music to special learners. In addition, I extend my gratitude once again to the following people who have helped me nurture my experience, talents, and gifts in public service to music education: Joseph and Clara Sugar, for their profound leadership and recommendation for me to serve as chairperson under past NYSSMA presidents: Peter Brasch, William Mercer, Richard Rabideau, Earl Groner (MENC Eastern President), and with association colleagues: Dr. Edward Marschilok, New York State Education Department; Elaine Gates, past president, Council of Music Teacher Education Programs; past and present administrators at the Board of Cooperative Educational Services of Nassau County, Department of Special Education; and family, friends, and colleagues who have contributed toward my positive outlook in all of life's challenges. I also wish to again express my gratitude to the American Biographical Institute (USA), Janet M. Evans, president, and the International

Biographical Centre (UK), Nicholas S. Law, director-general, for extending through their publications and jointly sponsored International Congresses, worldwide recognition for my contributions to society in the fields of special music education and performance. As with the first edition, this publication is dedicated to my sons, Marlon and Aaron, with love, forever and always.

Notes on the Second Edition

THE SECOND EDITION of *An Attitude and Approach for Teaching Music to Special Learners* reflects six additional years of member service to the music education community under New York State School Music Association past presidents John M. Krestic and James E. Orgar, current president James J. Cassara, and with president-elect Susan Weber; *School Music News* editor Thomas N. Gellert; parliamentarian Joseph Andreucci; and all members of the NYSSMA Executive Council.

The success of the first edition is attributed to the reader-friendly format of this text, original thought, and practical content based on my experience and training in the field. During my active tenure as the NYSSMA chairperson for music for special learners, we have seen positive change in our music teacher education-inclusion training programs, supportive legislation, and a much higher visibility for music in special education programs. My work has gone global and has reached special-learner populations on the continents of Europe, Asia, North and South America, Africa, and Australia, as well as New Zealand and the island of Aruba.

An Attitude and Approach for Teaching Music to Special Learners is used as a reference text at the university level. It has been included in the professional resource library of MENC: The National Association for Music Education since its first printing. With changes in education laws and the book's widespread use in college and school communities, revisions will be useful for practicing teachers. The reader will find in this new edition, published by Rowman & Littlefield Education in partnership with MENC: the National Association for Music Education, text updates, appendices of special education law updates, a listing and suggested use of frequently used books in the special education general-music classroom, a reference of print in text, a listing of author writings, several footnotes of newsworthy changes, and a thorough index. My gratitude goes to John Mahlmann, executive director of MENC, for taking the time to write encouraging notes each year in support of my service to music education. My thanks go to the marketing and publications team (Frances S. Ponick, director of publications, and Linda C. Brown, assistant editor, at MENC; Thomas F. Koerner, VP and editorial director, and Paul J. Cacciato, assistant managing editor, at Rowman & Littlefield Education) for sharing a global vision for this book, and finally my sincere thanks go to my college students who are a part of the forever-evolving process of teaching and learning.

This volume is dedicated to bringing the benefits and joy of music to *all* children, especially the most severely challenged, both young and old.

Elise S. Sobol
Melville, Long Island
New York, USA
July 2007

Using This Book

A KEY TO THE approach described in this book is the use of color, and most of the figures in the book incorporate color. All figures in the book are available for use in PDF format on the accompanying CD; those incorporating color are available in color on the CD to make this important feature available to you in the classroom.

The black-and-white figures in the book are coded to denote what colors are represented as follows:

G = Green (high)
Y = Yellow (middle)
R = Red (low)

The PDF files on the accompanying CD can be viewed with Adobe Acrobat Reader, which is available for free from the Adobe website (www.adobe.com).

The Basics

AEIOU's of Teaching Special Learners

The music room should be a happy place where all students feel safe, secure, and successful.

A-Assurance
E-Esteem
I-Interaction
O-Opportunity
U-Understanding
Y-You

ABC's of Vocal and Instrumental Adaptation

Vocal adaptation:

A. Use songs with limited range
B. Use songs with lots of repetition
C. Use songs that can be easily memorized.

1

Instrumental adaptation:

> A. Use tactile aids for string and wind instruments.
> B. Use visual aids for keyboard identification.
> C. Use color-coding for percussion: high-middle-low.

Classroom Setup

In setting up your music classroom, please keep in mind that all students need to feel equal. It is recommended that there be no front or back rows; rather, a horseshoe formation for chairs, with direct access to entrance and exit doors, instrument closets, audio equipment, and so on is preferable. There should only be minimal movement required for small-group activities. Students should be seated every other seat, if possible, so that a teacher or teacher-aide can sit in between to assist with behavior, and so that students are not threatened by close proximity. This idea should be adapted with a mainstreamed class—the special student should feel safe and secure with the seating arrangement.

Classroom Management

Clearly and simply state your classroom rules so that each student knows what is expected of him or her. For example, all students were multiply handicapped in one of the center-based special education facilities where I taught, and the rules for the music room were as follows:

> 1. Sit in your designated seat.
> 2. Ask before you touch.
> 3. Try your best.

Each student was assured that his or her best was different from every other person in the class, but every student could earn five checks each music class if he or she followed all the rules. These rules were adapted to each student's individual educational program (IEP) as part of a schoolwide behavior management program. Each musical activity was evaluated and assessed according to the needs of the particular student. The points earned in music class were transferred to the classroom teacher's record for each student. Total points for the week earned privileges for each student as an important part of their growth recognition. The students had the power of choice, and each choice had its positive or negative consequences.

Classroom Discipline

Clearly state rules and consequences. Have students be role models for other students by having a leader's chair. Have the leader's chair centrally located in the music classroom for all students to feel special when it is their turn to be the role model. Use cooperative learning techniques to foster positive interdependence between students. Use cooperative discipline techniques to foster a classroom with dynamics and mutual respect. A student will not become hostile or uncooperative if you make connections with acceptance, attention, appreciation, affirmation, and affection. In working with students with special needs, it is important to deal with the here and now, not yesterday. Reinforce the positive constantly. Use direct, nonthreatening suggestions for success. Each school district has a code of conduct. Know state and school regulations for extreme and disruptive students.

Foundations of Music Education
for Teaching Special Learners

Foundations of music education for teaching special learners is a teaching attitude and approach that will serve the teacher of general, vocal, and instrumental music in today's diverse school populations. It is a multimodal technique to ensure the successful inclusion and performance of students with specific learning disabilities; children from diverse backgrounds and cultures; those who are physically, mentally, psychologically, socially, and emotionally challenged; and the opposite side of the spectrum, the talented and gifted.

A Vocabulary of Special Education

To best understand this attitude, approach, and technique for inclusion, specific terms used in special education are explained below.

Exceptional

Exceptional is a term used concurrently with the phrase "special learners" to define those children whose school performance shows a significant discrepancy between *ability* and *achievement* and who, as a result, require special instruction, assistance, or equipment.

IDEA (Individuals with Disabilities Education Act)

The IDEA was formerly called Public Law 94-142 or the Education for All Handicapped Children Act of 1975. It requires public schools to make available to all eligible children with disabilities a free and appropriate public education in the least restrictive environment appropriate to their individual needs. Amendments were made to IDEA on June 6, 1997, to reauthorize and to make improvements. Please refer to Appendix A for updates in special education law.

FAPE (Free and Appropriate Public Education)

This term is used in Public Law 94-142, the Individuals with Disabilities Education Act, to mean special education and related services that are provided at public expense and conform to the state requirements and the individual's educational program.

IEP (Individualized Education Program)

The IDEA requires public school systems to develop an appropriate individualized education program (IEP) for each child. The specific special education and *related services* outlined in each IEP reflect the individualized needs of each student. Music educators need to be sure that if a student is mainstreamed into the music program, all accommodations applicable to the program are met for successful inclusion. If not, consult your department chair, special education chair, and administrator for direction and assistance.

Related Services

Related services may include in-school individual counseling, in-school group counseling, speech or language therapy, physical and occupational therapy, art therapy, adaptive physical education, music therapy, itinerant services for the hearing impaired, itinerant services for visually impaired, or a sign language interpreter. These services are in addition to the child's academic special education program and would encompass the opportunity for the student to be included in the school's general music classes and vocal or instrumental performance groups. The Committee on Special Education determines what related services the student will need to fulfill the specific individualized education program. If a suspected disability is not severe enough to warrant classification and services under IDEA (P.L. 93-112), Section 504 of the Rehabilitation Act of 1973 provides an alternative for a student to receive access to an educational program, the support of accommodations, or related services. For further discussion of this, please refer to the section on Laws against Discrimination.

Committee on Special Education (CSE)

The Committee on Special Education (CSE) consists of a team of knowledgeable persons who decide what related services a child needs to receive that will support the academic special education process. The team generally includes the child's teacher; parents or guardian; the child, if deemed appropriate; an agency representative who is qualified to provide or supervise the provision of special education; and other individuals at the parent or agency's discretion. This multidisciplinary team is established in accordance with the provisions of Section 5502 of the State Education Law—State Education Department Office of Vocational and Educational Services for Individuals with Disabilities (VESID).

Due Process

Due process is the timeline that starts when you suspect a child may need special services. It is date and time specific, requiring a series of tests to be performed prior to the formalized Committee on Special Education (CSE) meeting. The due process is designed to protect the rights of parents of individuals with disabilities. The formal and informal procedures are for implementation, review, and revision of an IEP.

Cognitive Functions and Dysfunctions

Cognitive function is a term that pertains to thinking skills or mental processes. *Cognitive dysfunction* is a term that is used by special educators to explain the different functioning of three phases of our mental processes: the input phase, the elaboration phase, and the output phase. The *input* phase is when the student takes in the information. *Elaboration* is the process where the brain defines a task, compares and integrates sources of information, plans, hypothesizes, and works through problems logically. The *output* phase is the skill of efficient, accurate, and appropriate communication. Students with dysfunction in any of the three phases may be considered special learners and may require *instructional adaptation* in how information is presented. (For further information see Skuy 1996.)

Instructional Adaptations for Learning

Instructional adaptations for learning are carefully planned procedures tailored to each specific need that will help the student reach optimal learning. Instructional adaptations should be applied to students with behavior disorders, the intellectually challenged, speech- and language-impaired students, those with sensory deficits, physical and health disabilities, the ethnically diverse, and the gifted and talented. Each adaptation should make the student feel safe, secure, and successful in the music room.

Please note that the State Education Department in each state works hand in hand with the U.S. Department of Education in issuing regulations and requirements for the basic education of all children with and without disabilities, impairments, or handicapping conditions. For questions and issues in your music program, please contact the liaison to music and the performing arts in your State Education Department as well as MENC: The National Association for Music Education for advocacy.

Definitions of Categories of Disabilities

In the State of New York, the State Education Department Office of Vocational and Educational Services for Individuals with Disabilities (VESID) issues the Part 200 Regulations of the Commissioner of Education. The Part 200 Regulations serve to define the designating categories of students who have been identified as having a disability and who require special services and programs. The following thirteen designations and definitions are included in the Part 200.1 section of Regulations of the Commissioner of Education, March 2000, pp. 12–14. This copyright-free information is essential information for the music educator. The following designations, listed alphabetically, and definitions are currently in use by national and New York State teachers.

1. *Autism*—a developmental disability significantly affecting verbal and nonverbal communication and social interaction, generally evident before age three, that adversely affects a student's educational performance. Other characteristics often associated with autism are engagement in repetitive activities and stereotyped movements, resistance to environmental change or change in daily routines, and unusual responses to sensory experiences.

2. *Deafness*—a hearing impairment that is so severe that the student is impaired in processing linguistic information through hearing, with or without amplification, that adversely affects a student's educational performance.

3. *Deaf-Blindness*—concomitant hearing and visual impairments, the combination of which causes such severe communication and other developmental and educational needs that they cannot be accommodated in special education programs solely for students with deafness or students with blindness.

4. *Emotionally disturbed*—a condition exhibiting one or more of the following characteristics over a long period of time and to a marked degree that adversely affects a student's educational performance:

    (a) an inability to learn that cannot be explained by intellectual, sensory, or health factors;

    (b) an inability to build or maintain satisfactory interpersonal relationships with peers and teachers;

    (c) inappropriate types of behavior or feelings under normal circumstances;

    (d) a generally pervasive mood of unhappiness or depression;

    (e) a tendency to develop physical symptoms or fears associated with personal or school problems.

    The term includes schizophrenia. The term does not apply to students who are socially maladjusted, unless it is determined that they have an emotional disturbance.

5. *Hearing impairment*—an impairment in hearing, whether permanent or fluctuating, that adversely affects the child's educational performance but that is not included under the definition of *deafness* in this section.

6. *Learning disability*—a disorder in one or more of the basic psychological processes involved in understanding or in using language, spoken or written, which manifests itself in an imperfectability to listen, think, speak, read, write, spell, or to do mathematical calculations. The term includes such conditions as perceptual disabilities, brain injury, minimal brain dysfunction, dyslexia, and developmental aphasia. The term does

not include learning problems that are primarily the result of visual, hearing, or motor disabilities; of mental retardation; of emotional disturbances; or of environmental, cultural, or economic disadvantage. A student who exhibits a discrepancy of 50 percent or more between expected achievement and actual achievement determined on an individual basis shall be deemed to have a learning disability.

7. *Mental retardation*—significantly subaverage general intellectual functioning, existing concurrently with deficits in adaptive behavior and manifested during the developmental period, that adversely affects a student's educational performance.

8. *Multiple disabilities*—concomitant impairments (such as mental retardation–blindness, mental retardation–orthopedic impairment, etc.), the combination of which causes educational needs that cannot be accommodated in a special education program solely for one of the impairments. The term does not include deaf-blindness.

9. *Orthopedic impairment*—a severe orthopedic impairment that adversely affects a student's educational performance. The term includes impairments caused by congenital anomaly (e.g., clubfoot, absence of some member, etc.), impairments caused by disease (e.g., poliomyelitis, bone tuberculosis, etc.), and impairments from other causes (e.g., cerebral palsy, amputation, and fractures or burns that cause contractures).

10. *Other health-impairment*—having limited strength, vitality, or alertness, including a heightened alertness to environmental stimuli, that results in limited alertness with respect to the educational environment, that is due to chronic or acute health problems, including but not limited to a heart condition, tuberculosis, rheumatic fever, nephritis, asthma, sickle cell anemia, hemophilia, epilepsy, lead poisoning, leukemia, diabetes, attention deficit disorder or attention deficit hyperactivity disorder, or Tourette's syndrome, which adversely affects a student's educational performance.

11. *Speech or language impairment*—a communication disorder, such as stuttering, impaired articulation, a language impairment,

or voice impairment that adversely affects a student's educational performance.

12. *Traumatic brain injury*—an acquired injury to the brain caused by an external physical force or by certain medical conditions such as stroke, encephalitis, aneurysm, anoxia, or brain tumors with resulting impairments that adversely affect education performance. The term includes open or closed head injuries or brain injuries from certain medical conditions resulting in mild, moderate, or severe impairments in one or more areas, including cognition; language; memory; attention; reasoning; abstract thinking; judgment; problem solving; sensory, perceptual, and motor abilities; psychosocial behavior; physical functions; information processing; and speech. The term does not include injuries that are congenital or caused by birth trauma.

13. *Visual impairment including blindness*—an impairment in vision that, even with correction, adversely affects a student's educational performance. The term includes both partial sight and blindness.

♪♪♪

Part 200 Regulations of the Commissioner of Education also includes definitions of the different special education programs for which students with disabilities may be eligible. These programs could be a transitional support service or a structured learning environment that offers a twelve-month special program and implementation of each IEP. The complete Part 200 regulations can be downloaded from the VESID website: www.nysed.gov/vesid. For specific inclusion issues and for sites and phone numbers of VESID regional associates in a specific school district that would interact with educators and parents, contact your state VESID website. For national information, start with U.S. Department of Education Office of Special Education and Rehabilitative Services (OSERS) www.ed.gov/about/offices/list/osers/index.html and follow links of interest.

♪♪♪

Talented and Gifted

Have you ever had students who you knew could perform better than the results showed? These students so often experience boredom and frustration in school because they struggle to "fit in," but the reality is that they need to feel challenged by intellectual inquiry and exhilarated by discovery and the gaining of knowledge through creating, composing, inventing, hypothesizing, designing, and synthesizing the world around them.

Section 902 of Public Law 95-561, The Gifted and Talented Children's Act of 1978, indicates that the term *gifted and talented* means children and, whenever applicable, youth who are identified at the preschool, elementary, or secondary level as possessing demonstrated or potential abilities that give evidence of high performance capabilities in such areas as intellectual, creative, or leadership ability or in the performing and visual arts. According to the U.S. Department of Education, their special abilities often require special attention and teaching techniques.

Music and the creative arts is an area where the talented and gifted student can excel. Their creative thinking and perfectionist tendencies, directed by an understanding teacher or mentor, can enable that precocious student to develop wholesomely. All music lessons, classrooms, and performances are recommended to be geared to the six steps of Benjamin Bloom's Taxonomy. Learning objectives need to follow a spiral-shaped curve that incorporates the following at each stage of development. These concepts are listed from the bottom to the top of the spiral.

6. Synthesis-Create
5. Evaluation-Judge
4. Analysis (Compare/Contrast)
3. Application
2. Comprehension
1. Knowledge

In order to raise a college student's disability awareness, this process is used in each of the undergraduate and graduate music education courses that I'm privileged to teach. Whether an article, book, or film is assigned, each college student is asked after reporting on the specific disabilities, disorders, or impairments to begin stage three of "applying the knowledge" to teaching in the music classroom. Class members work this application through to include the highest skills of cognition, synthesis of class activities that would apply the knowledge in new and creative ways. Direct teaching— just the giving out of knowledge—does not give the student tools for lifelong learning. Applying, analyzing, evaluating, and creating engages the total person to use his or her gifts of multiple intelligence to find the ultimate power of expression for contributions to self, class, community, state, nation, and world.

Twice exceptional students are characterized by being talented and gifted and also having learning, perceptual, physical, or behavioral problems. While challenging the students intellectually, effective teaching practices for the disability, disorder, or impairment need to be applied along with constructive discipline practices. It is absolutely imperative to remember: *if the student presents a danger to himself or to others, this needs to be brought to the attention of your direct supervisor, department chair, and administrators for further evaluation and action.* For further current reading, contact the National Education Association with the keyword: *twice exceptional.*

No matter what end of the spectrum your students are, activities in the music program can enhance their self-esteem. Feelings of self-worth are increased by the recognition of the valuable contributions in class that they can make. For the special learner with low cognitive abilities and problems in processing, a teacher is absolutely necessary to guide the student outcomes. For a talented and gifted group, peer interaction and contribution make class projects extraordinarily interesting and engaging for all. (See section on Teaching Critical Thinking Skills.)

Ethnically Diverse Students

In addition to the talented and gifted student and the student with special learning disabilities, children from diverse backgrounds and cultures present a different type of challenge to the music teacher. These students may face at least two sets of expectations: those of their home and those of the school. They may not be fluent in the English language and may experience communication difficulties. We are fortunate as music educators because music is a universal language. A tremendously interesting curriculum can be devised for a music program using international music, customs, dances, and folklore to enrich all students in a multicultural perspective. We are all a part of the universe—one (uni) song (verse). The following will serve as basic building blocks for development of teaching students from other cultures.

First and foremost, besides understanding that we are all a part of the one song (our universe), is understanding universal emotions. Ed Young in his *Voices of the Heart* (1997) invites all children young and old to explore the many voices from our hearts. The virtuous heart, the shameful heart, the understanding heart, the forgiving heart, the joyful heart, the sorrowful heart, the respectful heart, the rude heart, the contented heart, the despairing heart, the lazy heart, the able heart, the graceful heart, the forgetful heart, the resentful heart, the constant heart, the aspiring heart, the frightened heart, the merciful heart, the tolerant heart, the angry heart, the silenced heart, the evil heart, the doubtful heart, and the loyal heart. Mr. Young is an artist; he expresses his thoughts through Chinese characters and visual collage. As musicians we can teach these thoughts through the language of musical notation and sound. We can broaden the lives of our students by exposing them to pleasant sound experiences, starting with the magical sounds of nature. Tranquil ocean waves offer a sea of peace. Like the fetus in the womb, the protecting waters envelop and bring nourishment to the new life. There is a feeling of safety. Anger and aggression need not be displayed. The winds whistle, the brooks gurgle, the trees sigh, the horses neigh, the cats purr, the frogs croak, and the little lambs bleat. Quiet little musicians can be found in the tall summer grass waving in the breeze. There are fiddling crickets, buzzing bees, chattering squirrels, squealing mice, and trilling toads. All these are nice sounds, good sounds, pleasant to our ears (Sobol 1998).

Although the music one hears may be a little different, all ethnically diverse students have this common ground. All students have four basic needs to be met in music class and across the disciplines. This is described in Glasser (1982) and has developed into a theory for education called choice theory. A student will do well in school if he or she has a sense of

1. *Belonging.* Students need to feel accepted and welcome.
2. *Gaining power.* A student will grow in knowledge and skill and gain self-esteem through success. Through modeling a musical activity the student will gain power by successful mastery of that activity through realistic teacher direction.
3. *Having fun.* Having fun improves health, builds positive relationships, and enhances thinking. No matter how diverse the students are in the music classroom, activities need to have laughter. Students need to be uplifted and spirited to add to the quality of their successful program.
4. *Being free.* All students, disturbed, challenged, or gifted, mainstreamed or not, need to express control of their own lives. They need to set goals, make plans, choose behaviors, evaluate results, and learn from each experience to do things better (Sobol 1998).

In addition to filling the four basic above-mentioned needs in the music program for every student, the music educator should include music from past civilizations where, for instance, the universe was considered to be a world in balance with harmony. For the Chinese, music expressed a celestial order. For people in India, all things came from one sound, which entered both realms of the spiritual and the material. For the Greeks, music contributed to good health, curing illness of both the mind and body.

There are many sources on the market for learning more about multicultural education. Particularly helpful in shaping my attitude and approach to teaching music to special learners was the *World In Tune* Catalog. *World In Tune* is an integrated approach to world music, with music as the center linked to all other disciplines. This approach, recaptured from the ancients, is geared to stimulate student interest. Once an interest is aroused, the learning follows, and all students are engaged in the process because they *want* to be. Another helpful source is the *Culture Catalog—Multimedia Resources in Folklore, History, Culture, and the Arts* for integration across the disciplines. See the References section for contact information for these and other resources.

An up-to-date book filled with research on cultural and environmental factors that have shaped behaviors in specific populations is *Diverse Populations of Gifted Children: Meeting Their Needs in the Regular Classroom and Beyond* (Cline and Schwartz 1999). The authors cover characteristics of Asian Americans, African Americans, Native Americans, and Puerto Ricans. Each background may impact language, behavior and personal interactions, learning style, and values. Invite your students to share information about commonalities—festivals, flags, seasonal practices, and holidays. All can be united through music and the performing arts.

Remember that we live in one world. Let us share and learn from each other. Let us respect one another's dignity and be living proof and practice of the 1989 United Nations Universal Declaration of Human Rights. This declaration has been adapted for children. Of particular beauty for the music classroom is *An Adaptation of the Universal Declaration of Human Rights for Children*, a book available from the United Nations bookstore (Rocha and Roth 1995).

There has been significant progress recently in discovering the mysterious and remarkable functions of the brain. However, "no computer has yet come close to matching the capabilities of the human brain" (Berkow, Beers, and Fletcher 1997, 304). Life is full of countless variations, including different learning styles. Musical/rhythmic intelligence is a language-related intelligence that goes beyond cultural bias and words themselves. Music and the creative cultural arts are an essential key to the academic progress of all students, whether they are ethnically diverse, have special learning needs, or are gifted and talented. Music links our humanity to science, math, language arts, history, social studies, physical education, business, art, and drama. It is the center for our soul. Remember, the music room is to be a place where each and every student can feel safe, secure, and successful.

Disorders Requiring Educational Interventions

Developmental Disorders: Mental Disability

There are four categories of developmental disorders: educable, trainable, severe, and profound. The more severe the category, the greater the possibility of associated features being present (e.g., visual, auditory, or cardiovascular problems). Other educational implications involve poor social skills, severe academic deficits, and possible behavioral manifestations (i.e., low frustration tolerance, aggression, low self-esteem, and in some cases self-injurious behavior).

Pervasive Developmental Disorders: Autistic Disorders

This wide spectrum of developmental disorders also ranges in severity. It can be characterized by severe impairment in the development of verbal and nonverbal communication skills, lack of social skills, and almost nonexistent imaginative activity. Asperger's syndrome, infantile autism, fragile X syndrome, Kanner's syndrome, among other strains of autism have been identified by the scientific and medical community. With students with autism, educational implications include oppositional and aggressive behavior, seizures, low intellectual or very high intellectual development, poor social skills, and impaired cognitive functioning and language.

Specific Learning Disabilities

Dyscalculia-Mathematics Disorder. Dyscalculia is a serious marked disability in arithmetic skills that requires modifications such as extended time, use of a calculator, and revised test format. Poor self-esteem and social self-consciousness bring on avoidance and an increase of secondary problems. Dyscalculia often persists throughout the schooling years. It is not the result of mental retardation; inadequate teaching; or visual, hearing, or auditory deficits.

Disorder of Written Expression. Disorder of written expression is a serious impairment in the ability to develop expressive writing skills. It is also not the result of mental retardation; inadequate teaching; visual, hearing, or auditory deficits; or neurological dysfunction. A music teacher may recognize some symptoms of this disorder by seeing that the student has an inability to compose appropriate written texts and has serious and consistent spelling, grammatical, or punctuation errors. The student also may have poor organization of thought and to cover up the problem may exhibit a series of symptomatic behaviors including avoidance, procrastination, denial, and possible disruptive behaviors when a written assignment is given out.

Dyslexia-Reading Disorders. With dyslexia, a student has difficulty in decoding words and comprehension skills that significantly interfere with academic performance. "As with most developmental disorders, this condition is not the result of mental retardation, inadequate educational experiences, visual or hearing defects, or neurological dysfunction"(Pierangelo and Jacoby 1996, 182). In the *Parents' Complete Special Education Guide*, the reader will find listings of other pervasive developmental disorders that include expressive language disorders, phonological disorders, and receptive language disorders. Music teachers should be aware that according to the research of Pierangelo and Jacoby, 3 to 10 percent of school-age children suffer from expressive language disorder, which may greatly hamper a child's social interaction skills as well as academic performance.

The music room should be a people-friendly place, a happy place, a place where abilities shine and deficits are de-emphasized. What a student cannot say in language, he may say through music. Music is a language beyond words and transcends all educational systems and cultures.

Common Disruptive Behavior Disorders

Common disruptive behavior disorders are identified as conduct disorders and oppositional defiant disorders. With this type of disorder, success occurs when the student in the music program knows the boundaries for his behaviors. Make sure rules are clearly stated and easy to follow. Make sure consequences to rules broken are as clearly stated and faultlessly understood. Follow routine; address expectations of each activity or performance.

Anxiety Disorders

Common anxiety disorders of childhood are identified as separation anxiety disorder, avoidant disorder (child withdraws from social contact or interaction), and overanxious disorder (an excessive level of anxiety or worry over a long period of time). For instance, if a student shows withdrawal from being a leader of an activity or even volunteering where he has to pass out worksheets or instruments, etc., please tell him he will not fail and can feel safe. When he is ready, he can volunteer for leadership. Otherwise, praise all participation activities to enhance self-esteem, self-worth, and security of the child.

Physical Disabilities

Physical disabilities, of course, are caused by many different conditions. One of the more common physical disabilities you may encounter is cerebral palsy—a condition characterized by poor muscle control, paralysis, and other neurological deficiencies resulting from brain injury that occurs during pregnancy, during birth, after birth, or before age five (Berkow, Beers, and Fletcher 1997, 1429–30). There are four types of cerebral palsy: spastic, choreoathetoid (muscles spontaneously move slowly without normal control), ataxias (coordination is poor and movements are shaky), and mixed (a combination of two or more types together). Forty percent of children with cerebral palsy have normal or above normal intelligence. Speech is difficult for a child with cerebral palsy because the child has difficulty controlling the muscles involved in speech production. A child with cerebral palsy may also have epileptic seizures. If you have a child with cerebral palsy in your music program, get specific instructions for signs of a seizure in your student and what to do when it happens.

Above all, do not move the student. If possible note the time and duration. Report the seizure to the school nurse, immediately.

Limb Deficiency. Missing a limb from birth or losing one after birth due to accident or disease is another common physical disability. The acquisition of an artificial limb (prosthesis) can be important to the physical and psychological well-being of the individual.

Muscular Dystrophy. Muscular dystrophy is part of a group of inherited muscle disorders that lead to muscle weakness of varying severity. It is caused by a recessive gene that is carried on the X chromosome. It is a progressive disorder that eventually forces the child to become confined to a wheelchair. The different dystrophies, including Duchenne's and Becker's muscular dystrophies, differ in the expected life span of the child. Ninety percent of those with Becker's muscular dystrophy are still alive at the age of twenty, whereas those with Duchenne's are not (Berkow, Beers, and Fletcher 1997, 335–37). No matter how long or short the days, music can enhance the quality of living for your student with compromised physical abilities.

Spina Bifida. Spina bifida is a condition in which one or more vertebrae fail to develop completely, leaving a portion of the spinal column unprotected. The risk of having a child with spina bifida is linked with having a deficiency of folate (folic acid) when pregnant. Many physical complications can occur when a child has spina bifida. Physical therapy keeps joints mobile and strengthens muscles.

Down Syndrome

Down syndrome is a chromosomal abnormality. A person normally has twenty-three pairs of chromosomes. In a person with Down syndrome, there is an extra chromosome, making three of a kind, called trisomy. Both physical and mental development is delayed. In a person with typical development, the average intelligence quotient is considered to be 100. The average IQ of a person with Down syndrome has been shown to be in the range of 50. Physical characteristics (formerly called mongolism) are distinctive: a small head, broad face, flat slanting eyes, short nose, large tongue, small low-set eyes, and hands short and broad with a single crease across the palm. The pinkie often has only two sections instead of three and curves inward. A child with Down syndrome, like all children, has a tremendous capacity to appreciate music and the creative and the performing arts. The talents of a child with Down syndrome should be encouraged, as it will be the key to a successful and satisfying life. (For inspiration for teaching music students with Down syndrome, see the website of the multitalented instrumentalist Sujeet Desai, at www.sujeet.com.)

Cystic Fibrosis

Cystic fibrosis is a hereditary disease that causes certain glands to produce abnormal secretions, resulting in several symptoms, the most important of which affect the digestive tract and the lungs. It affects girls and boys equally (Berkow, Beers, and Fletcher 1997, 220–23). If a child in your music program has cystic fibrosis and starts to cough or gag, get medical attention immediately.

Infectious and Communicable Diseases

We have come a long way in curing once-incurable diseases, but today, there still are infectious diseases that school personnel, parents, and the community need to be aware of. They are chicken pox, cytomegalovirus (direct contact with blood or urine), gonorrhea (bodily fluids, blood, or vaginal fluids), hepatitis A (fecal-oral), hepatitis B (direct contact with blood), herpes I (above waist), herpes II (below waist), HIV infection/AIDS, measles, mononucleosis (saliva), mumps (transmission through sneezing), respiratory syncytial virus (RSV; nasal discharge), and salmonella bacteria (fecal-oral transmission) (Pierangelo and Jacoby 1996). Among the most common blood-borne infections of the liver is hepatitis C. Music teachers are urged to use universal precautions at all times with students. Have a school-approved disinfectant as well as antibacterial soap and facial tissues handy in the music classroom.

Visual Impairments

Lack of vision or reduced vision may result in delays or limitations in motor, cognitive, and social development. If you have a blind or vision-impaired child in your music program, you may be quite surprised at the enhanced musical ability present. Without visual stimuli from the environment, the ear becomes keener. With music this is a plus and can provide a positive outlet and bridge for academic progress and performance. A high proportion of students with visual impairments have additional disabilities and may require a curriculum that includes reading and writing in Braille, listening skills, personal-social and daily living skills, orientation and mobility, career education, and instruction in the use of special aids and equipment. Read the child's IEP and make sure you make all necessary accommodations in the music room. Then delight in having a very important addition to your chorus or instrumental ensemble. A wonderful resource for teaching music students with visual impairments is the Lighthouse Music School in New York City; refer to www.lighthouse.org.

Hearing Impairments

Hearing impairments may be a result of damage to the cochlea or the auditory nerve. This damage is caused by illness and disease (rubella, German measles, meningitis), RH incompatibility, heredity factors, exposure to noise, and certain antibiotics. The child with a hearing impairment can gain great enjoyment from music class by being part of a group and experiencing sound through feeling vibrations, movement, and dancing and communicating through finger and hand signs. Just like all children, there will be a large array of abilities among the hearing-impaired in your music program. If the IEP stipulates that your student have a sign interpreter for each class, make sure that covers the music class, too.

Eating Disorders

Serious eating disorders—anorexia nervosa, bulimia nervosa, or binge eating—are receiving special focus in schools across the country. Having an eating disorder impacts a student's ability to perform at his or her best potential. If you suspect a student in your music program of having difficulty in this area, bring this to the attention of the school psychologist, social worker, or nursing personnel.

Laws against Discrimination

Two federal laws have had an effect on school programs and facilities: Section 504 of the Rehabilitation Act of 1973 and the Americans with Disabilities Act of 1990.

The Rehabilitation Act of 1973 (P.L. 93-112)

The purpose of this act is to provide vocational rehabilitation services to handicapped individuals and prohibit discrimination on the basis of a disability by the federal government and federal contractors, by recipients of federal financial assistance, and in federal programs and activities. Applications to federally funded learning institutions of higher education can seek support services for people with disabilities who are not eligible under IDEA (Individuals with Disabilities Education Act). However, just as there is an IEP team for special education services under IDEA, there is a data-gathering process by a "504 team" to decide eligibility for a student to receive related services under Section 504. The Americans with Disabilities Act, passed in 1990, strengthened the accessibility of Section 504 to all public domains.

Americans with Disabilities Act (ADA)

Performing musicians, for example, are protected against discrimination in the workplace by the Americans with Disabilities Act (ADA). Enacted in July 1990, the ADA prohibits discrimination on the basis of disability related to employment, public services access, use of public accommodations, and access to public and private transportation services and telecommunications services. An individual with a disability is defined as a person who has a physical or mental impairment that substantially limits one or more major life activities, a person who has a history or record of such an impairment, or a person who is perceived by others as having such an impairment (U.S. Department of Justice 2005). The ADA does not specifically name all of the impairments that are covered. Title II of the act requires state and local governments to give people with disabilities an equal opportunity to benefit from all of their programs, services, and activities.

The Americans with Disabilities Act and its many sections help govern behavior and protocol. Interpretively it is also a guide for our music classrooms. It helps us always put the *person first*, not the disability. For in-depth information and the newest updates of the Americans with Disabilities Act of 1990 and related issues of Section 504 of the Rehabilitation Act of 1973, visit the U.S. Department of Justice website, www.ada.gov/pubs/ada.htm, and follow the various links for the information of interest.

Effective Teaching Strategies across the Disabilities

In 1996, MENC: The National Association for Music Education and Very Special Arts Educational Services developed a training program for music educators working with children with disabilities in regular education settings. For all categories of disabilities, it was recommended that the music educator have four components in an effective music lesson. (Adapted from Dark et al. 1996, 65.)

1. *Modeling.* Music teacher is to demonstrate a desired behavior before expecting students to perform the behavior.
2. *Introducing new information in small steps.* Music teacher should present the music activity by breaking it down to its components and then presenting the components one at a time.
3. *Multimodal and multisensory presentation.* Music teacher should present a single concept in a variety of ways (multimodal). Lesson

ıuld use audio-visual-tactile-kinesthetic techniques (multi-
ısory) for maximum student understanding.

4. *Clues to facilitate recall.* Music teacher should present new
   learning in ways that assist the children in remembering the
   information.

Throughout the years, experience, training, and skills have been
developed for teaching students with varying disabilities. Although
the following lists are by no means exhaustive, they should provide
the new music teacher with clues for teaching the diverse populations
in both urban and rural school settings.

Some instructional strategies used for teaching students with
learning disabilities include:

- Use highly structured activities with clear expectations.
- Communicate in short sentences using a simple vocabulary.
- Pace the class so that children are neither left behind nor bored.
- Provide immediate feedback and positive reinforcement.
- Recognize appropriate behavior by providing immediate praise.
- Recognize inappropriate behavior by giving constructive sug-
  gestions on appropriate behavior.
- Establish rules and consequences for inappropriate behaviors.
- Model positive attitudes—be what you want your students to
  become.

Some instructional strategies for students with behavioral
disabilities include:

- Maintain structure and standard routines in all aspects of the
  class.
- If change in routine is necessary, give students consideration
  and alert them to the change. Post the change, speak to the
  classroom teacher ahead of time to help prepare the student for
  change, give the student reinforcement for being flexible.
- Consider ways to modify the environment to minimize dis-
  tractions. When an activity is finished with one instrument,

collect the instrument, put it away, and then take out the next instrument.

- Give specific and immediate feedback to maintain positive reinforcement. Acknowledge students' needs at all times. Enlist the help of the students within the class to maintain classroom decorum.
- Have classroom rules clearly posted for easy reference. Be consistent and have a designated place in the room for a student who might need to take a constructive break from an activity.

Some instructional strategies for students with autism and developmental disabilities (a wide spectrum of cognitive abilities) include:

- Teach through modeling and imitation. Understand that a student with autism learns best by moving and doing.
- Use visual prompts to initiate behavior.
- Use timers constructively (in consultation with student's Functional Behavior Assessment—FBA).
- Plan for generalization (for example, every exit sign means the same thing).
- Maintain behavior with reinforcements (in consultation with special education team).
- Use token economy and point system.
- Use systematic attention and approval.
- Use planned ignoring where necessary to maintain classroom management.
- Build self-concept through praise for even the smallest accomplishments.

Some instructional strategies for students with attention deficit disorder with or without hyperactivity include:

- Teach and consistently reinforce social skills.
- Mediate asking questions.
- Define and redefine expectations.
- Assess understanding of content.
- Define and redefine appropriateness and inappropriateness.

- Make connections explicitly clear.
- Take nothing for granted.
- Enforce the positive.
- Define benefits of completing a task.
- Use lots of rehearsals to embed information into short-term memory.
- Clearly indicate on music score clues to recall rehearsal information.
- Establish support through creative seating to enhance student security.
- Post rehearsal plan.
- Repeat expectations that are realistic each session.
- Teach repertoire that enhances character development and self-esteem.
- Include twenty-first-century relevance.
- Be informed if a student receives medication to help boost his capacity to regulate impulsive responses. Plan student participation accordingly.
- Follow Classroom and Performance Program structure strictly so that students with attention deficits know the sequence "first," "then."

Some instructional strategies for students with physical, orthopedic, or other health impairments include:

- Make sure class matches requirements from student's IEP.
- Design lessons that build reduced or limited strength.
- Build motor skills (through consultation with goals of assigned occupational and physical therapists).
- Enhance vitality by building self-esteem through music.
- Ensure accessibility to and inside classroom or performance space.
- Make the environment safe and secure with intercom access to call for assistance in case of health alert.
- Look at what students can do and adapt musical instruments with materials such as Velcro to hold a triangle on wrist, to enhance student's ability to play.
- Use universal precautions for protection against infection.

Some instructional strategies for students with speech, language, and communication disorders include:

- With consultation with a speech therapist, use techniques to immediately assess their input, processing, and output in your music program.
- Use alternate means of communication such as a communication board and devices for effective responses.
- Use a microphone to build verbal response.
- Use lots of movement activities including signing to build cognitive understanding of music concepts and expression of language arts.
- Use teacher prompt to initiate response.
- Limit response choice for building strong communication.
- Model learning behaviors for building blocks of communication.

Some instructional strategies for students with hearing impairments include:

- Stand or seat student near the sound source.
- Use an FM amplifier for students with moderate hearing loss.
- Select instrument appropriate to range of hearing.
- Use visual strategies.
- Use signing.
- Use movement for the music.
- Use Windows Media Player, which dramatizes sound through artistic rhythm and design.
- Use instruments for feeling rhythmic vibrations.
- Use a keyboard that lights to the touch to match melody and harmony.

Some instructional strategies for students with visual impairments include:

- Enlarge print.
- Use contrasting colors, like white on black.
- Use music technology/transcription software.

- Use a Braille printer.
- Use tactile props.
- Use audio enhancement for visual directions.
- Use sequential learning to enhance memory.
- Record parts and lessons on tape.
- Create safety in space and place.

Some instructional strategies for students with emotional difficulties include:

- Maintain a pace conducive to kind respect.
- Champion challenge with role models.
- Use a wide spectrum of sound repertoire to develop optimum student expression.
- Ask individual student his or her specific needs.
- Implement Glasser's (1998) choice theory to interweave a student's physical and psychological needs of belonging, gaining power, having fun, and being free in the classroom.
- Make time for exploration and improvisation.

Overall, if a music teacher does not have the proper modifications to implement the requirements of the student's IEP, the teacher should ask the immediate supervisor for direction and assistance. Each school district is responsible for being in legal compliance with the obligation to serve the educational needs of every student.

Musical Process for Academic Progress

Introduction to Musical Literacy

To maximize learning for the student with special needs, concepts in music can be linked in a reality-based system that unites the worlds inside and outside of the classroom to build applications for successful living for each study. For example, as an introduction to musical literacy, let us look first at the symbol of the universal stoplight. The colors are red for stop, yellow for caution, and green for go. The world over, one sees this combination. Road signs are green; brake lights are red; yellow lines divide the lanes of traffic. As music teachers we can introduce these universal symbols to our students, building competence and confidence while developing a musical reading process. The upside-down stoplight (figure 2.1) can be used with the "Green-Red Song" (figure 2.2) to study high and low melodic pitches and with the "Green, Yellow, Red Song" (figure 2.3) for adding a middle tone. Ear training can begin with three different-sized bongo drums or

Upside Down Stoplight

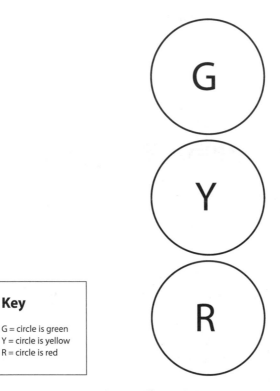

Key

G = circle is green
Y = circle is yellow
R = circle is red

Figure 2.1
Color version of figure can be found on accompanying CD.

tom-toms. Work on drums can then be transferred to xylophones and keyboards for work in tonic, thirds, and fifths. Students at first play the songs, responding aurally to teacher cues. Then the students gradually combine ear and eye coordination to perform without teacher assistance. This lesson can be combined with a basic classroom management technique described in Daniel Goleman's book *Emotional Intelligence* (1995, 276). The technique is called appropriately "The Stoplight Exercise."

Green   Red   Song

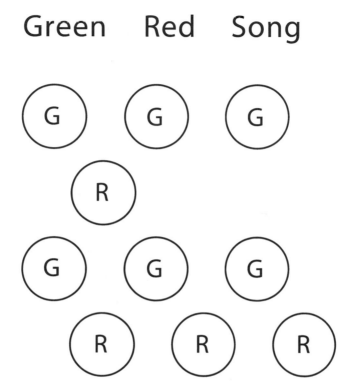

Key

G = circle is green
Y = circle is yellow
R = circle is red

Figure 2.2
Color version of figure can be found on accompanying CD.

Green Yellow Red
Song

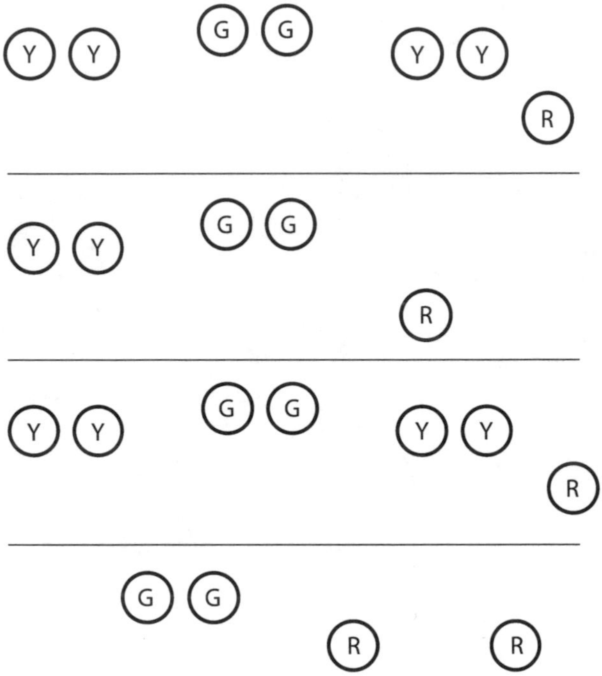

Key

G = circle is green
Y = circle is yellow
R = circle is red

Figure 2.3
Color version of figure can be found on accompanying CD.

The components of the Stoplight Exercise are:

Red Light:	1. Stop, calm down, and think before you act.
Yellow Light:	2. Say the problem and how you feel.
	3. Set a positive goal.
	4. Think of lots of solutions.
	5. Think ahead to the consequences.
Green Light:	6. Go ahead and try the best plan.

Having worked with students with severe psychological and emotional difficulties and currently with students with autism and developmental disabilities, I have found the stoplight notion offers a concrete set of steps for dealing with those momentous moments in the classroom. Beyond the management of feelings, it points a way to a more effective action. As a way of handling the unruly emotional impulse of thinking before acting, it becomes a basic technique for dealing with situations with school-aged children. This coupled with the red, yellow, green system of teaching foundations in musical literacy creates a win-win recipe for music in the special education classroom.

Class Structure—Sound Signals

On the open seas, sound and light signals are used to communicate directions. All military personnel understand these signals for navigation. Applying this principle to the music class, from the first introduction to red as a low tone and green as a high tone, the music teacher can establish directions for classroom management (figure 2.4). These signals are based on the way we speak.

Please stand up: low, low, high = red, red, green.
Please sit down: high, high, low = green, green, red.

Adding our middle tone, yellow color, we say,

Please get in line: high, high, middle, low = green, green, yellow, red.

Sound Signals for Classroom Management

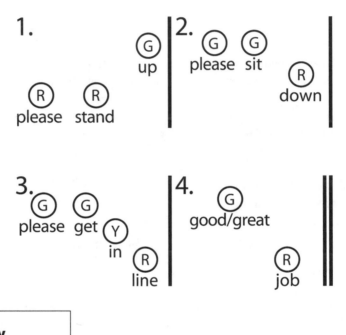

Figure 2.4
Color version of figure can be found on accompanying CD.

Bring closure to class by saying,

Good job: high, low = green, red.

Sound Signals to Melodic Understanding

Active music listening helps special learners build their ability to focus and concentrate. With a corresponding association, letters are to syllables as dots are to musical notes. Prereading skills of following the rhythmic pulse of words in a song can be combined with ear training for steps and skips in a scale as well as for numerical drills. Figures 2.5, 2.6, 2.7, 2.8, and 2.9 illustrate this process for the special learner. The classroom setup below shows a sign on the miniature piano that says "We Read From Left to Right," indicating the directionality of reading as well as for playing the steps of the scale on the miniature piano and on the drums pictured. This diagram serves as a visual cue for reading and playing skills. Humpty Dumpty sits proudly on the top of the piano to remind the challenged students

Figure 2.5
Color version of figure can be found on accompanying CD.

The red dots on drums 1 and 8 (and corresponding cards) identify the tonic or harmonic root of the C Major scale. The green dots on the drums 2–7 (and corresponding cards) indicate the melodic notes and steps of the C Major scale. Color version of figure can be found on accompanying CD.

Figure 2.6

Sound Signals to Melodic Understanding

Letters/Syllables = Dots/Musical Notes

Figure 2.7
Color version of figure can be found on accompanying CD.

Months of the Year

Key

G = circle is green
R = circle is red

Figure 2.8

How Many Syllables?
(sounds)

How Many Notes?
(dots)

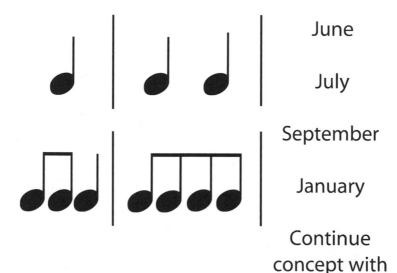

June

July

September

January

Continue
concept with
all 12
months

Figure 2.9

"all the kings horses and all the kings men *work together* to put Humpty together again." Next to the miniature piano is a chart with song words to be mastered.

In figure 2.6, the single-pitched bongo drums are arranged in an octave scale, low to high, left to right, in a pattern with labeled index cards representing the numbers of the dots on the drums. The dots serve to reach across the diverse student population. Some students may not yet be able to read the American number system because in their own culture they work with an abacus. So, the dots serve as a tactile representation of our number system. The four pictures in figure 2.6 show the tuned drums, with the red dots on drums 1 and 8 denoting C, and the green dots on drums 2–7 indicating the melodic notes and steps of the C Major scale. The drums are used for progressing step-by-step through the drills in figures 2.7 through 2.9 with the accompaniment of the music teacher on the piano.

- First, students play the drums with the numbers 1–8 shown in dots alone (learning number concepts and hearing the steps and skips). Depending on the level of the students, the numbers can be used to discuss the steps, skips, and musical intervals.
- Next, number cards are added in front of the drums (learning number symbols and hearing steps and skips). Students now are reading "dots" and number symbols.
- Then, number cards with corresponding dots are added. Skills are further reinforced as students match the dots on the drums to the dots on the number cards.
- Finally, students play using the cards with the names of the notes in front of the numbers—the last stage to learning the notes while playing melodies using the steps, skips, and letters.

Working with the tuned bongo drums helps the gross motor skill development of our students, especially for those with physical and occupational therapy goals on their IEPs. This listening, playing, hand-eye coordination process has been shown to enhance cognitive function for these prereading skills.

Figure 2.7 shows again the Sound Signals to Melodic Understanding in the "Days of the Week Song." Students can follow the melody of the song by tapping the drums to the words and matching the pitches of the song with the appropriate scale step. The teacher plays the song on the piano and gives direct instruction to the students. Pitch is learned by ear training and singing. Students work with their own personal copies of the color-coded song. Touching the words of the songs as they sing helps students to feel the rhythmic pulse of each word. Every student has a chance to play the bongos and touch the dots and words on the big song charts. Depending on the number of students in the class, taking turns can be done at the end of every phrase or the entire song. Key to success is that every student is actively engaged at all times during the lesson.

Figure 2.7 concludes with the word "Saturday." Our voices naturally drop at the end of the word "Saturday"; this is indicated by the red dot on the tonic.

In figure 2.8, "The Months of the Year Song" builds on phonemic awareness of the sound syllables in each month. Again the song ends on the tonic, naturally following the voice tone of the word "December."

Figure 2.9 is the end of the process—students with learning disabilities can successfully match the names of the month with the dots, which are now written in musical notation. This step-by-step, audio-visual-tactile-kinesthetic approach to learning musical notation establishes a relationship between musical sound discrimination and the tonality of speech in song and literacy.

Depending on the level of the students, the teacher can link learning to language arts, math, science, social studies, physical and health education, drama, art, business, and technology curricula through creative melodic drills. Identify the seven letters of the musical alphabet with number dot cards. Transfer the concept of the seven letters of the musical alphabet to seven days of the week, seven wonders of the world, seven colors of the rainbow, seven tones of the diatonic scale, seven chakras or energy systems in our body, seven dwarfs in *Snow White*, and so on.

Introduction to Rhythmic Notation

Figures 2.10, 2.11, 2.12, and 2.13 show a visual illustration of a conceptual way to introduce the reading and decoding skills of rhythmic notation. Along with a story, the illustrations show the relationships between music and math with a consistent use of the red, yellow, green color applications.

The rhythm of a song is the heartbeat of the music. For special learners this can first be described by doing a motor activity: stop (whole note), stand up (half note), walk (quarter notes), jog (eighth notes), run (sixteenth notes). A descriptive story can follow like this:

> In the Beginning there was only One sound (figure 2.10). All sounds lived in this One sound. There was so much sound in the One sound that the Whole note had to divide. When a whole note divides it grows a stem. When a half note divides it gets colored in. When a quarter note divides it grows a flag. Two flags join together with a beam, and so forth (figure 2.11).

Rhythm drills consistently use green and red notes, this time to signify fast and slow rhythms (figure 2.12). Link song syllables to rhythmic pulse in learning choral works and for identification of repertoire in games such as "Name That Tune" (figure 2.13). The music teacher can demonstrate a train moving from slow to high speed through the correlation of rhythm. To keep consistent relevance to these ideas, the teacher can compare formations that birds fly in the sky with formations of marching bands on the football field, and so on.

Reading Notation on a Staff

Using figure 2.14, students are instructed to either fold or draw lines connecting the two horizontal dots so that we have a picture of five lines and four spaces. While doing this, the music teacher should link the math concept that the distance between two points is a line. Place dots (reading from left to right) from bottom to top (feet to

In The Beginning
There Was
One Sound

Green
Red
Yellow

Figure 2.10
Color version of figure can be found on accompanying CD.

Introduction to Rhythm

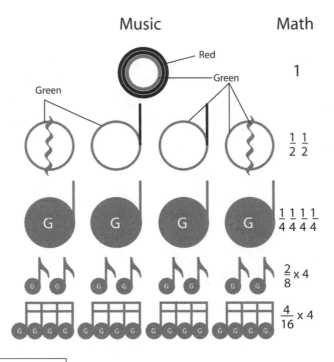

Figure 2.11
Color version of figure can be found on accompanying CD.

Rhythm Drills

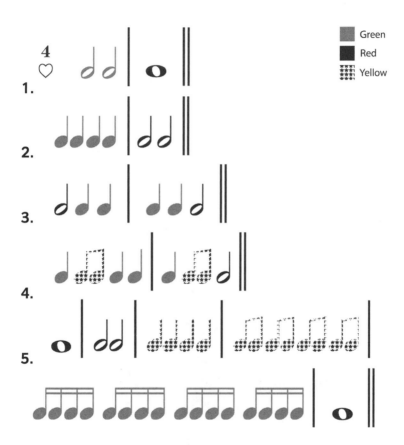

Figure 2.12
Color version of figure can be found on accompanying CD.

Name That Tune

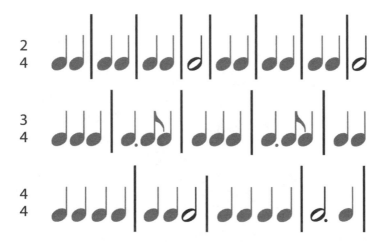

$\frac{2}{4}$ Twinkle, Twinkle, Little Star

$\frac{3}{4}$ My Country 'Tis of Thee

$\frac{4}{4}$ Old MacDonald Had a Farm

Figure 2.13
Color version of figure can be found on accompanying CD.

head), first line, first space; second line, second space; third line, third space; fourth line, fourth space; fifth line, fifth space. Arrange dots in an ascending line. Show the manual staff by pointing out how to count the lines and spaces on one's hand. Ask students for simple addition of five plus four equaling nine. Then link musical theory of inversion of intervals with the nine planets of our solar system and their lines of orbit and the harmony of ternary triads. Preliminary study of numerology shows that nine symbolizes our three worlds—body, intellect, and soul. It symbolizes eternity, completion, and incorruptibility. It is a number sacred in Christianity. In Judaism, it is the number of truth. *Jiu* (nine) is the number of eternity in Chinese tradition and a celestial number whose importance outshines all others. Indian mandalas are based on multiplications of nine, symbolizing the universe. Prior to September 2006, we were taught that our solar system was made up of the following nine known planets named from the nearest to the sun to the farthest away from the sun: Mercury, Venus, Earth, Mars, Jupiter, Saturn, Uranus, Neptune, and Pluto. On September 14, 2006, the *New York Times* reported that Pluto was demoted in status, given number 134340 in the catalog of minor planets, and planet Eris was elevated in status (figure 2.15).

The ancients believed that the universe was in harmony if it was in tune. For the people of India, all things come from one sound, Aum (Om), entering both realms of the spiritual and the material. For the Greeks, music contributed to good health, curing illnesses of both mind and body. A quick review of the story: In the beginning there was a whole note. The world was one. All sounds were one. As shown in figure 2.10, in the beginning there was One sound, which became the Music, literally and figuratively, for our whole Life.

Applications to Choral and Instrumental Programs

Literature for both choral and instrumental performance ensembles should be carefully chosen for special learners to gain self-esteem

Reading Notation on a Staff

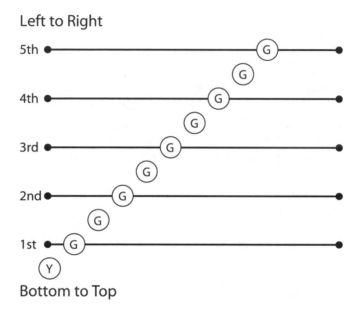

Left to Right

5th

4th

3rd

2nd

1st

Bottom to Top

Key

G = circle is green
Y = circle is yellow
R = circle is red

Figure 2.14
Color version of figure can be found on accompanying CD.

Uni-verse
One Song #9

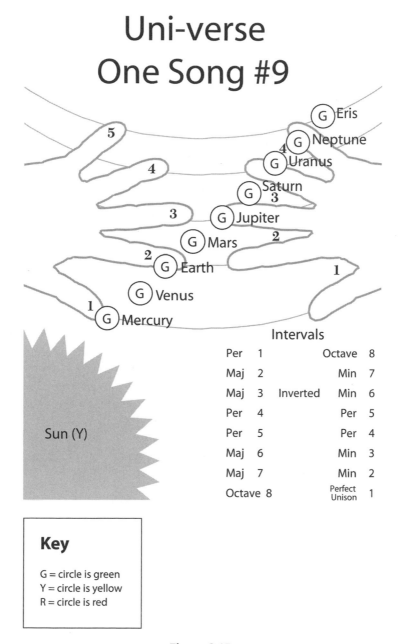

Figure 2.15
Color version of figure can be found on accompanying CD.

and competence. The work should have a universal and global message in its expression of emotion, demonstration of contrasts, and overall form of characterization and dramatization. While studying world music literature, we want to embrace the cultural diversity of the new Americans. At the same time, we also want to celebrate aspects of American culture through our own music by studying Native American music and great American composers, including Scott Joplin, Stephen Foster, Leonard Bernstein, Aaron Copland, Walter Piston, Karel Husa, Alan Hovhaness, and John Philip Sousa, to name a few. Create alternate special ensembles for choral literature and alternate special ensembles for instrumentalists, for example, with keyboards, choir chimes, steel drums, mariachi ensembles, and ethnic instruments. This can be *the* draw to maintain interest, develop confidence, and build socialization skills for all learners.

Success for Students of All Challenges and Learning Styles

When the special music educator can present his musical concepts in a multisensory mode that combines *auditory, tactile, visual, and kinesthetic feedback,* he or she reaches learners of all capabilities. The musical/rhythmic intelligence activates whole brain learning. It serves to link our humanity to science, math, language arts, history, social studies, physical education, business, art, dance, drama, and theater, building a bridge for success to students of all challenges and learning styles.

♪ THREE ♪

CHAPTER

The National Standards for Music Education

National Standards for Music Education[1]

There are nine national content standards for music education and learning in the arts, adopted in 1994:

1. Singing, alone and with others, a varied repertoire of music.
2. Performing on instruments, alone and with others, a varied repertoire of music.

---

1. From *National Standards for Arts Education*, Copyright © by MENC: The National Association for Music Education. Used by permission. The complete National Arts Standards and additional materials relating to the Standards are available from MENC: The National Association for Music Education, 1806 Robert Fulton Drive, Reston, Va. 20191 (www.menc.org/resources). For general background and the importance of National Standards for Arts Education see the link for the U.S. Department of Education (www.ed.gov/pubs/ArtsStandards.html).

3. Improvising melodies, variations, and accompaniments.
4. Composing and arranging music within specified guidelines.
5. Reading and notating music.
6. Listening to, analyzing, and describing music.
7. Evaluating music and music performances.
8. Understanding relationships between music, the other arts, and disciplines outside the arts.
9. Understanding music in relation to history and culture. (MENC 1994)

A good music lesson is well rounded and reaches our diverse populations with current relevance. All music educators should be familiar with their own state's expectations for implementation of the arts standards. As a music educator in New York State, my own experience is that the New York State Education Department (NYSED) urges and expects all teachers in the state to use learning experiences of highest value for the development of their students. Lessons should engage students' interest and press them toward growth and learning. Lessons should be easily adaptable to other classroom disciplines and clearly adaptable to students with different kinds of learning challenges. Lessons should have value beyond the classroom. The nine national standards are consolidated into four New York State Standards for Learning in the Arts (Dance, Music, Theatre, Visual Arts) as follows:

Standard 1: Creating, performing, and participating in the arts.
Standard 2: Knowing and using arts materials and resources.
Standard 3: Responding to and analyzing works of arts.
Standard 4: Understanding the cultural dimensions and contributions of the arts. (NYSED 1996)

Criteria for assessment and evaluation have been given by the New York State Education Department for students with and without severe disabilities, and teachers in that state should contact NYSED for proper assessment practices and coordinate efforts with their school district. The same or similar processes should be followed in each individual state.

For working with students with moderate to severe learning disabilities, experience has shown that the integration of whole language activities in the music classroom and mediated learning experiences in the special education and inclusion classroom are two approaches that can enable the music teacher to reach the standards for all students in his or her program. Examples follow.

Whole Language Activities through Music

In teaching music to special learners, whole language activities using music in listening, speaking (singing), reading (notation), and writing (composing) creatively touch all four standards with even the simplest of themes.

Whole language is a four-pronged approach. It encompasses listening, speaking, reading, and writing. These four elements are found in music. A music student can:

1. Increase his attention span through guided listening experiences.
2. Speak through vocal and instrumental expression.
3. Develop reading ability through graphic representation of sounds through music notation, traditional and otherwise.
4. Develop creative writing abilities by making up songs from story content and organizing curriculum concepts in rhythm and rhyme.

There are many assets to this program:

1. The student's day is more integrated from class to class through organizing themes.
2. Students are empowered to take responsibility for their own education.
3. Learning is student centered.

4. Teachers are life-long learners giving vibrancy to every single exchange.
5. Teachers evoke joy through their work, allowing students to excel to the best of their potential.
6. Music becomes life itself, instruction to the mind as well as to the heart.

The following whole language charts (figures 3.1–3.4) were designed for my teaching in the center-based special education setting for students with moderate to severe learning disabilities.

Mediated Learning in the Special Education and Inclusion Classroom

During the summer of 1999 I spoke about teaching music to special learners at the combined American Biographical Institute and International Biographical Centre Twenty-Sixth International Congress on Arts and Communications in Lisbon, Portugal. I was approached by the renowned Israeli conductor Dalia Atlas, who felt that I should meet Reuven Feuerstein, PhD, the founder and

Letters/Syllables
as
Dots/Musical Notes

Figure 3.1

Letters make words like "Go" and "Stop."

Dots make notes that Beat like a clock.

Figure 3.2

Syllables form words to make good sense.

Notes form rhythms which sound an event.

Figure 3.3

Whole Language Activity

- Whole note divides into two half notes.
- Two half notes divide into four quarter notes.
- Four quarter notes divide into eight eighth notes.
- Eight eighth notes divide into sixteen sixteenth notes.

- A Half Note is a Whole Note with a Stem.
- A Quarter Note is a Half Note Colored In.
- Eighth Notes wave a flag out from the Stem.
- Two flags mean Sixteenth Notes faster then.
- Beams connect a single or double flag.
- Dot after a note adds plus one.

Figure 3.4

director of the International Center for Enhancement of Learning Potential in Jerusalem. Atlas felt that I was practicing MLE (Mediated Learning Experiences) in the music classroom and that I could learn a great deal from Feuerstein. Additionally, Atlas felt that my work in the music classroom would be of interest to him. Feuerstein and I have been in correspondence during the past eight years. As soon as time allows, a trip will be arranged for me to present my ideas of using MLE in the special education music classroom for his colleagues at the International Center for Enhancement of Learning Potential in Jerusalem.

In 1999–2000, I ran a mediated learning pilot project with my challenged students at the special education elementary program where I was teaching. Mediated learning is a process by which the teacher helps severely challenged students get the desired result through techniques that enhance learning potential. The approach of MLE is demonstrated here in an action plan for Todd[2] as well as a detailed six-week lesson plan for using mediated learning techniques to enhance musical literacy as well as ear training. Mediated learning techniques are used while addressing the New York State Learning Standards for Students with Severe Disabilities. The New York State United Teachers (NYSUT) Effective Teaching Program graduate class Mediated Learning in the Special Education and Inclusion Classroom gave me the specific tools to set up this action and six-week lesson plan.

I am delighted to report that from the onset of the mediated learning class, my special education classes benefited from the mediation process on multiple levels. As a result of the techniques used, all 176 students were able to improve their cognitive responses in the music classroom. Their behaviors improved consistently since I immersed myself in becoming proficient in the methods and materials of mediated learning.

Each of the twenty-four special education classes had three rules for the music classroom:

---

2. Name has been changed to protect privacy.

1. Sit in the designated seat
2. Ask before you touch.
3. Try your best.

All classes had students with severe social, emotional, psychological, or learning disabilities. I found that with more mediation, fewer problems occurred. Rule 1 kept order when the classes made a transition to the music room. By putting a red dot on the seats designated for students, there were almost no errors when the students would enter my room. Without the red dot, it seemed that day after day, the students would get out of their line order, and get confused over who was first, second, third, and so on. Valuable time was lost getting each class seated. With the red dot posted beside Rule 1 outside on my rule sheet and the red dot on the back of each student chair, the students had a simple guide, and they were able to achieve success in getting seated at the beginning of class. The first student in line merely sat in the first red-dot chair, and so on for the other students in line.

Rule 2 was instituted because, since many of the students suffer from complications of attention deficit hyperactivity disorder (ADHD), their hands often did touch without permission and there were discipline issues. Further reinforcement of proper behavior regarding playing musical instruments during an activity helped achieve intentionality and reciprocity.

Rule 3 held the students responsible for understanding their activities, enabling them to try their best. Encouraging their own thinking kept their interest, kept them engaged in the learning activities, and made them quite proud of their achievements, no matter how large or small.

One particular eight-year-old boy we shall call Todd showed some remarkable improvements in the music classroom over the pilot six-week MLE lesson plan.

Todd had severe behavioral problems. He was oppositional. He would threaten violence. He had poor concentration. He had low frustration tolerance. He was impulsive. He was easily distracted. He was quite moody. He had poor social skills. He had perceptual motor deficits. He had moderate to severe attention-deficit problems and had shown suicidal tendencies. When faced with work that he felt was too difficult, he became angry and verbally abusive. All this aside, he had shown me during the three years that I was his music teacher that he was interested in excelling in every music class. He had a smile that lit up the room and a strong rhythmic sense that helped other students excel. Building strength upon strengths, he showed real delight in learning. I was thrilled when he could play the red-green songs and even more thrilled when he led the class in following the musical dots of Tchaikovsky's *Nutcracker* "March." Not only did Todd show hand-eye coordination, he was able to highlight the musical movement on the page by choosing the bright yellow marker. After he highlighted the notes on the page, he could then play them on the keyboard, transferring up and down, steps, skips, and repeated notes with directionality on the keyboard. Another area of excellence was shown in ear training. He was able to comprehend the story of the *Nutcracker* and recognize seven tunes from the ballet. For a normally functioning eight-year-old student, this is a good achievement; for Todd and his peers, it was extraordinarily exciting.[3]

Sample Lessons

MLE uses a step-by-step thinking process. The words related to this process are italicized in each step in the following sequential lessons.

Lesson One

- Target Skill: High and low in sound and space
- Age Range: Special education students ages five to ten adapted to twenty-four different classes with different disabilities

---

3. Practicing teachers have asked why I specifically chose the *Nutcracker* for this mediated learning experience plan. The answer is that at the time our school PTA was bringing in a local ballet company to perform it for our students during the holiday season. Therefore, in order to prepare my classes for their upcoming assembly program, I matched the repertoire in the music program classes.

- Time Range: General music class meeting twice a week for thirty minutes
- Mediated learning techniques used while addressing New York State (NYS) Standards for Students with Severe Disabilities

1. Creating, Performing, and Participating in the Arts: Intentionality and Reciprocity

Students will be introduced to high and low pitch through size analysis of instruments. Students will conclude through creative discovery that the large-size instrument has the lower pitch and that the smaller instrument has the higher pitch. The mediator will help guide the student's ability to categorize similar instruments by size and draw specific and general conclusions about sound.

2. Knowing and Using the Arts: Meaning

The mediator will direct students to understand that this musical concept is scientifically based. Experiments will be conducted with unpitched rhythm instruments and pitched instruments, including makeshift instruments such as flowerpots, seedpods, coffee cans, and rubber bands, as well as the string families, woodwind families, brass families, and percussion families.

3. Responding to and Analyzing Works of Art: Transcendence

The first lesson opens up to the students a new way of seeing that is critical to understanding the cultural dimensions in the arts. The students will apply the multisensory style of seeing, touching, and feeling to each new challenge. They will begin to understand specific voice ranges of instruments based on the size of the instruments. They will begin to understand written notation and the placement of notes in the staff for high and low pitches (directionality). By looking at a drum set they would know the order of the different drums and cymbals with application of the size-sound concept. Socially, the students will begin to hear differences in their sound environments. Emotionally, the students will expand their understanding of stimulus and reactions within their world. High and low will become important tools in their cognitive growth.

4. Understanding the Cultural Dimensions and Contributions of the Arts: Competence, Sharing, Individuation, Goal-Setting, and Challenge

With knowledge, students can feel competence. This lesson fosters competence, sharing, and individuation. The long-term goal is to enhance listening skills through music activities and bridge the ability to focus in other subject areas.

As music education lessons progress and the students start to learn to create melodies from different sounds and harmonies from stacking sounds, students will be repeatedly challenged to discover sound where he or she would not have listened before.

This primary lesson of discovering that the small instrument has the higher pitch and the large instrument has the lower pitch has brought safety, security, and success to each student. This self-change will serve the student as a tool for problem solving in different situations. "Do you hear what I hear?" "How do you know it is what you say?" "Shake it, strike it, pluck it—what has the higher pitch and why?" "How do you know that that is a train whistle and not a fire engine signal?"

Lesson Assessment Using Alternate Performance Indicators for Students with Severe Disabilities

+ = Frequently
/ = Evident
0 = Developing

Students will be assessed three ways. (1) Teacher will direct response through class demonstration. (2) Teacher will play a similar basic ear training tape or CD and record individual students' responses to questions of high and low sounds from audio recording (Sobol,

Name of Student _____Date_____			
1. Teacher will direct response through class demonstration	+	/	0
2.Teacher will record student response to high/low pitches from audio tape/ CD	+	/	0
3. Students to perform simple high/low songs with red dot and green dot on Tone bells, maracas, hand drums	+	/	0

Figure 3.5

E. S., *Ear Training for Children*, Side l, available from the author). (3) Students follow color code of red for low and green for high and perform simple high-low songs on tone bells, maracas, and hand drums. Student response will be kept in individual class folders. Figure 3.5 shows a sample rubric.

Lesson Two

- Target Skill: Same sound/different sound
- Age Range: Special education students ages five to ten adapted to twenty-four different classes with different disabilities
- Time Range: Part of a six-week plan, general music class meeting twice a week for thirty minutes
- Mediated learning techniques used while addressing the NYS Standards for Students with Severe Disabilities

1. Creating, Performing and Participating in the Arts: Intentionality and Reciprocity

Students will differentiate between same two-note pattern and different two-note patterns on the same instrument. Students will differentiate between same two-note pattern and different two-note patterns on instruments of different timbres (piano, violin, bell, drum, and guitar). This lesson is bridged to teaching about directionality in music. Students will learn to differentiate sounds going up (ascending) and going down (descending).

2. Knowing and Using the Arts: Meaning

The mediator will help build the students' vocabulary in the sound environment. Same and different sounds will be spoken, sung, and played. This is a very important beginning of a life-long concept in music education for musical literacy as well as in adaptive daily living.

3. Responding to and Analyzing Works of Art: Transcendence

Whether in music, art, dance, or theater, concepts of *same* and *different* are paramount and fundamental for building success. Throughout history, comparisons connect people around the world. Signals on the open seas are universal by sound. Sound creates meaning and meaning creates communication.

4. Understanding the Cultural Dimensions and Contributions of the Arts: Competence, Sharing, Individuation, Goal-Setting, Challenge, and Self-Change

The ear-training activities form a basis for all students to focus and distinguish. It bridges their language arts, sciences, social studies, math, and physical education. Same note and different note are pre-reading music skills. These bridge to letters, numbers, and signs. At this stage of development in the music class, I have used this lesson to introduce a structure for my classroom discipline. "Please sit down" is translated into musical pitches on high, high, low: 5-5-1. "Please stand up" is low, low, high: 1-1-5. "Please get in line" is high, middle, step, down: 5-3-2-1. And this lesson begins to form concepts of melody and harmony, concepts universal throughout the world, while establishing order in the classroom.

Lesson Assessment

+ = Frequently
/ = Evident
0 = Developing

Students will be assessed on same and different by *Ear Training for Children* (Side 2) in three ways. (1) Students will write *S* for same and *D* for different on a prepared worksheet. (2) Students will play color-coded simple melodies with red and green for same, different, high, and low. (3) Students will create their own same-different songs and have their peers perform them in class with the student composer as conductor.

This lesson builds on the student's success from Lesson One and adds to their competence and self-esteem. Student work will be kept in individual class folders and behavior kept on index cards arranged by class.

Lesson Three

- Target Skill: Rhythm in sound
- Age Range: Special education students ages five to ten adapted to twenty-four different classes with different disabilities
- Time Range: Third part of a six-week plan, general music class meeting twice a week for thirty minutes
- Mediated learning techniques used while addressing the NYS Standards for Students with Severe Disabilities

1. Creating, Performing, and Participating in the Arts: Intentionality and Reciprocity

This lesson reveals to the students that all things living have a rhythm. Play, hear, and feel your heart beat. What is your name? Is it Bill? That has one sound. Is it Mary? That has two sounds. Is it Patricia? That has three sounds. This is next in the series of ear-training activities. From first names to last names to full names, students can show their listening skills by playing on rhythm instruments, singing, and notating the rhythm. This lesson is bridged to teaching about tempos in rhythm.

2. Knowing and Using the Arts: Meaning

From identifying one-, two-, three-, or four-beat rhythms, students can extend their vocabulary and sound banks by starting to hear accents, or stressed sounds, in contrast to unaccented, or unstressed, sounds. Whatever the classroom, a lesson in this music concept can correlate to its content. Study of fruit—a student can categorize the fruits by sound. Pear—one sound; apple—two sounds; pineapple—three; watermelon—four sounds. These sounds will then be turned into musical symbols, necessary prereading skills.

3. Responding to and Analyzing Works of Art: Transcendence

The students in the program where I taught this project were all below grade level. They each had tracking problems in math and reading. This performance activity enabled each student with the instrument of his or her choice—drum set, hand drums, maracas, or bells—to perform a small story in sound. Each could play the rhythm of the song and then perform the rhythm of the words of the song. These are two different activities that go hand in hand and transcend to an ability to process what is heard and to improve overall academic performance in school.

4. Understanding the Cultural Dimensions and Contributions of the Arts: Competence, Sharing, Individuation, Goal-Setting, Challenge, and Self-Change

Universally, people's competence grows with familiarity. This lesson is a beginning activity in growing familiar with the sounds around us, acoustic natural sounds, and sounds of civilization. The sounds have an order. This order forms the basis for language development and is heard in melodies. Rain, ocean, summer nights, waterfalls, giggling, and crying are just a few of the sounds that have a rhythm and a pattern that become identifying characteristics. For this activity and the sophistication of the students, rhythms of sound were confined to the language arts program and its vocabulary of words, which students should know by the time they leave the program. Through group class projects, the students perform their compositions, clearly identifying rhythm—in music, speech, and language—while at the same time teachers can broaden their students' sound environments by assessment activities such as the one given below.

Lesson Assessment

> + = Frequently
> / = Evident
> 0 = Developing

Through echo-response activities all students will be assessed on their improved abilities to differentiate sounds and syllables. This will serve to improve their aural processing and help them throughout their education in listening, following directions, and auditory processing.

Lesson Four

- Target Skills: Reading notes on a musical staff
- Age Range: Special education students ages five to ten adapted to twenty-four different classes with different disabilities
- Time Range: Fourth part of a six-week plan, general music class meeting twice a week for thirty minutes
- Mediated learning techniques used while addressing the NYS Standards for Students with Severe Disabilities

1. Creating, Performing, and Participating in the Arts:
Intentionality and Reciprocity

This lesson introduces lines and spaces that comprise the musical staff on which a clef is placed to denote the name of each line and space. Correlation of lines and spaces is shown on one's hand—the fingers the five lines and in between the lines are the spaces. Students are guided through drills to identify a note on a line or in a space. Then students are shown the G clef, which names the second line of the staff as G (treble clef) following the musical alphabet of A, B, C, D, E, F, G up the staff (going higher) and down the staff (going lower). Lessons 1, 2, and 3 are reviewed so that the students can clearly demonstrate the step-by-step process of reading and writing notes on a music staff. Other clefs are introduced briefly—

the F clef, which is for bass clef, and the various C clefs, which names middle C where the clef is placed.

2. Knowing and Using the Arts: Meaning

Musical literacy is a wonderful way of giving confidence to a special learner. Is the note on a line? Is it in a space? Does the melody go by steps, or skips? The reading skills are rooted not in a rhyme but in the placement of the clef. Playing the notes on a keyboard helps with reading skills because the notes become visual as they ascend or descend. Adding right hand and left hand helps both sides of the brain develop as eye and hand coordination is added to cognitive development.

3. Responding to and Analyzing Works of Art: Transcendence

Musical notation is a sign for sound. Just as the written word gives freedom of expression to the writer, so too the notated note gives freedom of expression to the composer. It is this element, besides the element of interpreting others' ideas, that is so exciting to the special learner. His or her abilities can shine in composition—the structure of the language is not as complicated as that of English. The musical alphabet is limited to seven letters, not twenty-six or more. The staff has five lines, with ledger lines that can be added to make the sounds extend higher or lower. Just like reading books, reading musical notation gives the performer the freedom to discover music from all cultures and periods of history.

4. Understanding the Cultural Dimensions and Contributions of the Arts: Competence, Sharing, Individuation, Goal-Setting, Challenge, and Self-Change

Although the students I taught are just beginners in learning how to read a note on a musical scale, they can delight in games of putting words together from the musical alphabet and figuring out how to write them on the musical staff on the blackboard. They feel good as they gain confidence in writing the notes and the corresponding English letters that identity both worlds to them, language and music. The students could share in compiling name lists. The students could set goals to how many words they could think of. The students with severe learning disabilities are challenged in spelling but they are able to assess not only their own development in the music activity but their classroom behavior during the music class. Writing, reading, speaking, composing, and performing enhance the individuation of each learning experience to the benefit of each student and each class.

Lesson Assessment

+ = Frequently
/ = Evident
0 = Developing

Students will be assessed in three areas. (1) All students will complete worksheets that will show the teacher whether they can name the lines and spaces in the treble clef. The worksheets will show the student's understanding of high and low notes on the treble clef and the corresponding placement of the notes on the piano keyboard. (2) Students will compose a simple four-bar melody on the treble-clef staff with the assistance of the teacher. (3) Students will play their own melodies on the piano keyboard.

Lesson Five

- Target Skills: Finding patterns in music
- Age Range: Special education students ages five to ten adapted to twenty-four different classes with different disabilities
- Time Range: Fifth part of a six-week plan, general music class meeting twice a week for thirty minutes
- Mediated learning techniques used while addressing the NYS Standards for Students with Severe Disabilities

1. Creating, Performing, and Participating in the Arts: Intentionality and Reciprocity

Through reviewing familiar songs that the students know well, students identify two patterns by ear and body percussion, by letter and pencil and paper, and by echo and response. One pattern is from a song starting with the chorus first, then the verse, such as "Tingaleyo." The second pattern is from a song with the verse first, then the chorus, such as "Eye of the Tiger." Eight different songs are categorized with the intention to move ahead and teach the "March" of the *Nutcracker* suite, their first song of the year that has no words.

2. Knowing and Using the Arts: Meaning

Lesson Five uses skills learned in all previous lessons. What is the meaning of a pattern? Where do you find patterns? How does a pattern help with the structure or architecture of a piece of music? Can you tell the form of a piece knowing its pattern?

3. Responding to and Analyzing Works of Art: Transcendence

Guided listening experiences offer the best mediation possible for learning the different styles of music as well as learning the patterns of each individual piece, be it a simple song, a sonata, fantasia, or fugue. The identification of the components makes for a greater understanding. With greater understanding, mastering a composition becomes an exciting adventure. It is like having a tour guide give a minute-by-minute commentary on the sights you are seeing.

4. Understanding the Cultural Dimensions and Contributions of the Arts: Competence, Sharing, Individuation, Goal-Setting, Challenge, and Self-Change

From a song to a ballet, from words to a story without words, from sneakers to toe shoes, the six-week plan of lessons was geared to open the door of opportunity for the special education students to see a professional ballet company perform a traditional ballet, *The*

Nutcracker by Peter Ilyich Tchaikovsky. The goals were to have these severely challenged students first regulate their behavior in a large auditorium filled with the entire school, students, and staff, and second, to follow the story, keeping focused for an hour.

The patterns for familiar songs led to the patterns of the new music of the "March" in the *Nutcracker*. Every time they heard the music—since the experience was guided by hand clapping and patting activities, reading the notes, playing the notes—the students' interest was engaged. A video of the ballet was shown prior to the dance company's performance. In this technology-oriented society, students are used to watching a screen rather than interacting with each other. The video helped them prepare for the live version of the *Nutcracker*. Mediating through a multisensory style of teaching reached all the students. The outcome of the live performance raised the standard of task focus by 99 percent. The ballet was a truly successful experience for the students in this special education program.

Lesson Assessment

> \+ = Frequently
> / = Evident
> 0 = Developing

All students will show without teacher direction and through body percussion the patterns of eight familiar songs. Students will clap on the theme of the song and pat the verse of the song. Teacher will then play a completely unfamiliar song and students will have to discover through repeated listening the pattern of the song. For lower-level classes, teacher will model response. For middle- and higher-level classes, students will discover the pattern through guided questions of clues for listening.

Lesson Six

- Target Skills: Name the tune in *Nutcracker*
- Age Range: Special education students ages five to ten adapted to twenty-four different classes with different disabilities

- Time Range: Sixth part of a six-week plan, general music class meeting twice a week for thirty minutes
- Mediated learning techniques used while addressing the NYS Standards for Students with Severe Disabilities

1. Creating, Performing, and Participating in the Arts: Intentionality and Reciprocity

As a follow-up activity for seeing *The Nutcracker* ballet, all students will see if they can recognize at least five out of seven of the tunes from *The Nutcracker*.

The tunes presented were (1) "March," (2) "Arab Dance," (3) "Chinese Dance," (4) "Dance of the Reed Flutes," (5) "Russian Dance," (6) "Dance of the Sugar Plum Fairy," and (7) "Waltz of the Flowers." The process is teacher-directed for the name of the melodies as well as the spelling of the titles as the students find the letters they recognize. All tunes recognized are a great achievement for these special learners. Two out of seven, one out of seven, three out of seven, all is a stretch for the kids and an exciting result of MLE.

2. Knowing and Using the Arts: Meaning

Each dance was given a visual image for the students to connect with. Each dance was played repeatedly with the name given to prepare students to take the plunge and guess the name of the tune on their own, without assistance.

3. Responding to and Analyzing Works of Art: Transcendence

Learning seven tunes from the ballet and seeing how the costumes fit the movement of the dance and how the scenery changed with the story all enlightened the students. It also awakened them to an area of beauty that some would never have experienced. Other great works of music literature can be presented to the students now that this presentation was such a great success.

4. Understanding the Cultural Dimensions and Contributions of the Arts: Competence, Sharing, Individuation, Goal-Setting, Challenge, and Self-Change

As music teacher and as cultural arts coordinator at the center-based special education program where I taught, my hopes were to continue to present the finest in music, dance, art, and theater to the students with special learning needs so that they could find their own individual voices for creative expression. The arts enhanced all aspects of their learning.

Lesson Assessment

> \+ = Frequently
> / = Evident
> 0 = Developing

Students will show in whatever medium they choose to demonstrate to the teacher their understanding of *The Nutcracker* by Tchaikovsky. For their final evaluation they could sing, they could play an instrument, they could draw a scene. Expectations were individualized and praise was given to all as the utter success of the six weeks of lessons culminated in an inspiring musical experience for the students in this Long Island center-based special education elementary program. A rubric was drawn accordingly to reflect assessment of individual final-class projects.

Let's Talk about the Positive: Autism

For almost two decades I worked with students with severe learning disabilities and social, emotional, psychological, and behavioral issues. Due to a program downsizing, I was then transferred to a school for students with autism and developmental disabilities. The current statistics on numbers of children with autism is staggering (see www.autism-society.org). Autism is a spectrum disorder, meaning that the symptoms and characteristics of autism can present themselves in a wide variety of combinations from high-functioning and mild to severe. Individuals with autism may have other disorders that affect the functioning of the brain, such as epilepsy, mental retardation, or genetic disorders discussed earlier in this text.

As a music educator I have benefited from hearing the brilliant scientist Temple Grandin speak of how difficult it was for her as a child to sing and beat the drum simultaneously. Experience now has shown that students with autism and developmental disabilities learn best by doing. All lesson topics should be presented in an audio-visual-tactile-kinesthetic format with step-by-step procedures.

At the program where I teach presently, the students with autism and developmental disabilities ages eight to twenty-one are thriving in chorus, alternate instrumental ensembles, and weekly general music classes. Without a doubt, teaching students with autism and developmental disabilities is rewarding. The students are often very musically gifted, with near or perfect pitch, with the ability to learn even the most challenging music by rote and repetition. The opportunity to work with a student with autism is an opportunity for tremendous professional and spiritual growth. In many cases, the sensory impairment—unusual reactions to physical sensations, for example, being overly sensitive to touch or underresponsive to pain—are balanced out by enhancements in sight and hearing. Teach with a highly structured education and behavior program geared to what the student *can* do. Work closely with the classroom teacher and related and support personnel for optimal success in the music room.

Inspirational reading to the class may include the new book about heroes in the field *Different Like Me* (Elder 2006). The book has brief biographies of Albert Einstein, Dian Fossey, Glenn Gould, Hans Christian Anderson, and Temple Grandin to name a few of the personalities. Please refer to the section in this text on instructional adaptations for teaching students with autism and developmental disabilities.

Let's Talk about the Positive: ADHD and ADD

Some of the most challenging, difficult, and gratifying special learners are those who are diagnosed with attention deficit disorder

(ADD) or attention deficit hyperactivity disorder (ADHD). The distinction between ADHD and ADD is as follows: A student with ADHD has ADD and is hyperactive. This means he or she finds it very difficult to sit still and tends to wiggle, fidget, and squirm a lot. Hyperactive people have an incredible amount of energy and are always on the go. A student with ADD has trouble paying attention and concentrating. The command center of the brain, which tells other parts of the brain what to pay attention to and what to ignore does not work completely on target. There is a neurological inefficiency and chemical imbalance in the parts of the brain that control impulses, sensory input, and focusing of attention. Sometimes the brain of a person with ADD fails to tell the other parts of the brain what to ignore, so that a person with ADD might think listening to someone tapping a pencil is just as important as paying attention to what the teacher is saying. ADD is usually inherited, but the condition can also come from a brain injury or lead poisoning. So a student who has ADD is not necessarily ADHD, but a student who has ADHD has the conditions that a student with ADD has and is also hyperactive. It is important to understand that there may be other disorders in the student with ADHD and that all students need to be considered as separate cases. Rather than dwell on the negative aspects of teaching a student with ADD or ADHD, it is of more value to talk about the positive aspects of a student having ADHD.

With proper classroom techniques to increase attention, improve listening skills, build organizational and study habits, control impassivity, balance excessive activity levels, and develop immature social skills, a music teacher can find that his or her ADHD student is accepting, creative, empathetic, energetic, forgiving, gregarious, intuitive, innovative, inventive, imaginative, inquisitive, resourceful, resilient, risk-taking, sensitive, and spontaneous. Many of these gifts are seen in extraordinarily gifted and talented personalities and our greatest leaders. These qualities provide a vibrancy to the music classroom. For further information about learning disabilities contact the Council for Learning Disabilities (CLD), the Learning Disabilities Association of America (LDA), and the National Information Center for Children and Youth with Disabilities (NICHCY), which provide free information on disabilities and disability-related issues. See the References section for contact information.

Teaching Special Learners
Critical Thinking Skills

The following champion-of-challenges curriculum project is appropriate and adaptable for upper elementary through high school and continuing education programs. It addresses the standards in the arts while using standards in language arts, science, math, and social studies. The composers chosen are just an example of five of the many musical personalities and composers who have overcome their personal circumstances and developed greatness. This project was developed initially as part of the NYSUT (New York State United Teachers) Effective Teaching Program in Critical Thinking in which I took part in August 1997. I have used this project not only in the special education classroom but also in the undergraduate and graduate music education courses I currently teach. It is wonderful to help students learn through their own study how prominent musicians handled their own particular setbacks, persevered through difficulties, and as a result earned a distinct place in history. The words of Aldous Leonard Huxley always ring in my ears, "Experience is not what happens to you, it is what you do with what happens to you."

The first years of teaching in an alternate public education center-based special education program involved students from over fifty school districts, five to ten years of age. All the students had multiple social, emotional, and learning disabilities. Some of these students came from good caring and educated parents. Some of these students were in foster care, hoping for some loving parent to adopt them. Some students knew who their parents were, and some students had little knowledge of their parentage. Some students had siblings who lived with them, and others had siblings who were sent to different homes. Some students had above-age IQs, and others were below average. Some students could go back to their home school districts after receiving the support services. Others sometimes needed an even more restrictive environment such as a psychiatric hospital setting or a residential setting.

To varying degrees, the description of the students above can now be found in every school setting. All students have the same needs in common: to be loved, to be accepted, and to be given an opportunity through trained professionals to succeed to the best of their abilities. Through studying the lives of prominent musicians who have had their own challenges to conquer in their childhood, it was and is my goal to positively impact the students through music and help them gain strength over their own unique social, emotional, and educational development. With knowledge and skills to interpret the information, these students, even at the most primary level, can extend their own potential and surmount their own difficulties. A project like this can take up to six weeks with music classes meeting twice a week. The end product of the project would be for the students to create their own web of their lives, which would be a beautiful testimony to their enhanced self-esteem. In the long term, students would remember and recall when needed the stories that helped them to grow and to make a positive contribution to the lives of others.

Ludwig van Beethoven

Data presented to children:

- Born: December 16, 1770, Bonn, Germany
- Died: March 26, 1827, Vienna, Austria
- Parentage: Had a very mean drunken father who beat him to force him to practice the piano. Father wanted son to be a famous prodigy like Mozart.
- Childhood: Life for Beethoven was very hard. He began to go deaf when he was only about twenty-six years old. He became gruff and cross. He didn't have many friends.
- Outcome: Despite handicap and his constant financial struggles, Beethoven is considered one of the most important classical composers of all time. His notable works included nine

symphonies, the *Moonlight Sonata*, and "Für Elise." Despite his total deafness, not being able to hear a note of what he composed, one of his last compositions, the Ninth Symphony, included "Ode to Joy," a testimony to his triumph and peace at the end of his life.

- Music examples for students include "Ode to Joy," the *Moonlight Sonata*, the *Emperor Concerto*, and "Für Elise." Excerpts adapted for each class. Students will view insightful video *Beethoven Lives Upstairs*.

Giuseppe Verdi

Data presented to children:

- Born: October 9, 1813, Le Roncole, Italy
- Died: January 27, 1901, Milan, Italy
- Parentage: Verdi's parents ran a small inn and sold groceries in a little Italian town called Le Roncole. They sacrificed things for themselves in order to buy Giuseppe an old spinet piano.
- Childhood: Giuseppe showed great musical talent. One day he was putting some notes together to form chords; he found a chord that he liked very much. When he tried to find this chord again, he could not do so, and he flew into a childish rage. He grabbed a hammer and began to smash the precious piano. His father stopped him just in time before the piano was destroyed.
- Outcome: With time, Verdi grew out of his childish rages and produced some of the greatest operas ever written including *La Traviata, Il Trovatore, Otello*, and *Aida*. He died a national hero.
- Music examples for students include: *La Traviata*, Act 1, Scene 1; "Grand March" from *Aida*; "Anvil Chorus" from *Il Travatore*.

W. C. Handy

Data presented to children:

- Born: November 16, 1873, Florence, Alabama
- Died: March 28, 1958, New York, New York

- Parentage: Father was a minister and thought any music outside of the church was sinful.
- Childhood: Family was quite poor. W.C. worked hard at many odd jobs and gave his parents part of his earnings, saving a portion for himself. W.C. made music himself by humming through a comb wrapped in tissue. He wanted a guitar, saved his money, and bought it. His father forced W.C. to take the guitar back. His father insisted that W.C. become a minister, but W.C. never lost his dream of writing and playing music.
- Outcome: One day a cornet player in the circus sold him a cornet. This was the turning point of his life. He played with the Florence, Alabama, band, then stayed with music through good and bad times. He formed his own band and publishing company. He became blind, but continued to write music to the end of his life. His nickname was "Father of the Blues."
- Music examples for students include W. C. Handy's two greatest songs: "St. Louis Blues" and "Memphis Blues."

Louis Armstrong

Data presented to children:

- Born: August 4, 1901, New Orleans, Louisiana
- Died: July 6, 1971, Corona, Queens, New York
- Parentage: Parents separated, lived with his mother.
- Childhood: Louis Armstrong struggled against poverty and hard times in his early years. He broke the law at age thirteen by firing a gun to celebrate New Year's Eve. He was sent to jail, then to what was called "The Colored Waif's Home for Boys." It was a reform school for boys in trouble. As it turned out, opportunity came to him at the Waif's Home, and he was asked to join the Waif's Home Band, where he learned to play the cornet. He was allowed to leave the home after one year and return to his mother. He quickly became established as the best trumpeter around.

- Outcome: Louis Armstrong is remembered as the "Ambassador of Jazz." His lovingly popular nicknames were "Satchelmouth" or "Satchmo."
- Music examples include Disney songs, Satchmo-style original recordings of "Hello, Dolly" and "What a Wonderful World."

George Gershwin

Data presented to children:

- Born: September 16, 1898, Brooklyn, New York
- Died: July 11, 1937, Beverly Hills, California
- Parentage: Born in Brooklyn of loving parents. Second of four children.
- Childhood: As a young boy, he had little interest in music, reading, writing, or arithmetic. He loved sports, particularly baseball. This all changed around the age of fourteen when his family acquired a piano. Whole new worlds opened up to him. He surrounded himself with music and became a schooled musician who studied constantly—composition and piano lessons. At fifteen he left school and worked full-time as a "song plugger," playing the tunes of hopeful composers in Tin Pan Alley. He read all he could about the great musical personalities. He learned to play many instruments so that he might further his knowledge of orchestration. Through his incredible hard work, he was soon a published composer and together with his older brother, Ira, wrote many songs. George Gershwin suffered incredibly with headaches. He died tragically of an inoperable brain tumor.
- Outcome: George Gershwin brought jazz to a major level and to new audiences. Famous works include the opera *Porgy and Bess*, *Rhapsody in Blue* (first symphonic work using jazz music), and Concerto in F. The Academy Award–winning film *An American in Paris* (1951) was set to Gershwin's music.
- Music examples include: "Someone to Watch Over Me," "Oh, Lady Be Good," excerpts from *An American in Paris*, "I Got Rhythm," excerpts from *Rhapsody in Blue*.

Sample Unifying Questions for Study

All students will be divided into cooperative groups, and teacher and teacher assistants will guide each group with the questions. (For the initial project the complex of students had low cognitive abilities and learning disabilities in processing. Therefore, cooperative groups at times needed to be facilitated by an adult.) Students will devise a visual organizer in the shape of a five-pointed star and choose five things of importance to remember about each prominent musician.

Each group will present their own star with the composer's name in the center of the star.

1. Where was your composer born?
2. Describe the home environment of the composer/performer you studied.
3. What influences affected his or her childhood and his or her study of music?
4. Despite challenges, each personality studied is world renowned. What will you remember about the lives and music of the great men of music that we studied?
5. Indicate favorite musical example on top of your "star."

Figure 3.6

Visual Organizers are Arranged in Chronological Order

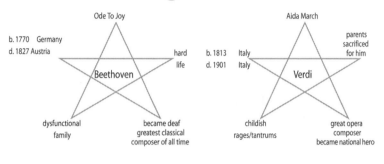

Ode To Joy

b. 1770 Germany
d. 1827 Austria

hard life

Beethoven

dysfunctional family

became deaf
greatest classical composer of all time

Aida March

b. 1813 Italy
d. 1901 Italy

parents sacrificed for him

Verdi

childish rages/tantrums

great opera composer
became national hero

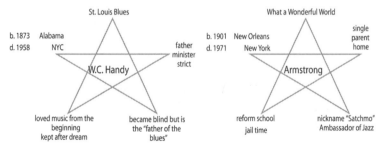

St. Louis Blues

b. 1873 Alabama
d. 1958 NYC

father minister strict

W.C. Handy

loved music from the beginning
kept after dream

became blind but is the "father of the blues"

What a Wonderful World

b. 1901 New Orleans
d. 1971 New York

single parent home

Armstrong

reform school
jail time

nickname "Satchmo"
Ambassador of Jazz

Someone To Watch Over Me

b. 1898 Brooklyn, NY
d. 1937 Beverly Hills

Supportive family

Gershwin

disliked school, loved sports
collaborated later with brother

influential jazz composer
influenced by classical, theater and movie

Figure 3.7

Relevant Applications for Student Success

Students will devise their own stars about themselves.

1. One point will have a favorite song.
2. One point will have their birth date and place.
3. One point will have something about their parentage.
4. One point will have something about a difficulty or disability.
5. One point will have something about an aspiration or ambition, "I want to be . . . ."

Follow-up activities for young children will include studying contemporary musicians in the rap, pop, folk, rock, and fusion styles. Further study will also include looking at famous musical stories and their characters, thinking creatively and critically about the life of Peter and the Wolf, Hansel and Gretel, Peer Gynt, and Billy the Kid. The focus in all cases will be to key into problem solving so that students find in fact and fiction how many ways there are to look at a situation and how many ways there are to solve a problem.

In all cases the students will organize the facts by making a timeline or web or other visual organizer. In the end through this process, wisdom will be gained and the best lesson they could learn from the music room is "Although I have such and such a problem, I can still become . . . ." "I want to be remembered as . . . ." This project can be taken and adapted to special learners of all ages. Five quotes to interpret on the higher level would be:

> "Any composer's writing is a sum of himself, of all his roots and influences."—Leonard Bernstein, composer and conductor
>
> "Success is not success if it affects personal attitudes."—Ira Gershwin, songwriter
>
> "Do what you can, with what you have, where you are." —Theodore Roosevelt, twenty-sixth president of the United States

"Music can serve as a way of capturing feelings, knowledge about feelings, or knowledge about the forms of feelings."
—Howard Gardner, leading cognitive psychologist

"Music is your own experience, your thoughts, your wisdom. If you don't live it, it won't come out of your horn."
—Charlie "Yardbird" Parker, jazz legend

♪ FOUR ♪

CHAPTER

International Speeches

Communication through Music:
A Language beyond Words Presented at The
ABI/IBC International Congress on Arts and
Communications, Lisbon, Portugal, July 15, 1999

Good morning. Last night's gala concert included me performing *Ten Variations on an Air of Gluck* by W. A. Mozart and an arrangement of Cole Porter's *Night and Day*. Being a music teacher for special learners, I can attest that these two composers can be heard from a different perspective. They each faced extreme challenges in their lives. Mozart, supremely gifted, had a childhood that was spent performing and living "on the road." By biographical account, he was a sickly, frail child who suffered from vague diagnoses and questionable treatments. When Mozart wasn't traveling, he was ill. It was a vicious cycle, all of which contributed to his many life difficulties, his kidney failure, and early death at age thirty-five.

Cole Porter, on the other hand, represents another kind of genius. He kept his extraordinarily painful disability from a horseback riding accident from his adoring public. He loved traveling, and especially enjoyed exploring the *fado* (folk music) of Portugal and visiting that country's many famous windmills. But frequently, due to physical pain, his friends would have to carry him when he couldn't use a wheelchair or the support of his canes.

In Nassau County, Long Island, where I am employed as a music teacher for children with special needs, the children have extreme social, emotional, psychological, and behavioral problems with learning disabilities. Their age range is five to ten. My most important function is to bring them to a happy place in music where they feel safe, secure, and successful. These children need assistance to help them find a place of peace when they feel bad, angry, hurt, troubled, or sad. Some of the children are from good homes; some of them have no homes, and live in a residential facility. Some know their parentage; some do not. Some are born with chemical imbalances due to prenatal drug or alcoholic conditions. Some are born with health impairments that interfere with them having a regular routine. Some have inoperable tumors; some are fighting terminal illnesses. But all of these children are someone's son or daughter, someone's hopes and dreams. They deserve to be loved and given every opportunity to develop their potential.

For students with shattered lives, it is important to show that life is full of beauty. This is demonstrated by introducing to them the music of past civilizations, when, for instance, the universe was considered to be a world in tune with harmony. For the Chinese, music expressed a celestial order. For the Indian, all things come from one sound, entering both realms of the spiritual and the material. For the Greeks, music contributed to good health, curing illnesses of both mind and body. Great civilizations rise and fall but are all connected by the universe—uni (one) verse (song). All children heard their mother's heartbeat in the womb. They heard summer night noises, mountain springs, spring rain, and ocean waves. In my classroom, as a beginning study in the beauty of life, the students have a chance to play replicas of ancient instruments while hearing sounds of nature. This begins to form a sound bank of good, calm sounds, where energy can be refocused; where the student can begin to feel sunshine and warmth and not be afraid of the dark. [Demonstration includes use of acoustic relaxation machine and instruments.]

For the children who have been in and out of foster homes, awaiting the possibility of adoption, the song "The Earth Is My Home" gives them a sense of belonging, purpose, and plan of action. Please follow me in singing this song with sign.

> The Earth is my home, The Earth is my home, The Earth is my home. I promise to keep it healthy and beautiful. I will love the land, the air, the water, and all living creatures. I will be the defender of my planet. United with friends. I will save the Earth. (KSE 1991)

Special learners can see a world of wonder challenging us to extend our own human potential. The artist Sarah Perry (1995) marvelously illustrates this wonderment in her book, *If*. Five examples from this book are "If frogs ate rainbows"; "If kids had tails"; "If toes were teeth"; "If ugly were beautiful"; and the reason why I purchased the book, "If music could be held" [seen on overhead projector].

For me, music can be held. Listen for a moment to the following selection of George Hamilton Green's *Triplets*. The xylophone soloist is Evelyn Glennie, who is considered the world's greatest percussionist. Evelyn Glennie is deaf. She is quoted as saying that her deafness is something unique and that she treasures it. It is something she says has even helped her. Ms. Glennie is the perfect segue for me to teach my students about the life and works of Ludwig van Beethoven and his struggles to deal with not only his abusive home life but later a life of increasing deafness. The tool I use is the tuning fork. This way my students can hold the music (feeling of vibrations) and are empowered by their new understanding of the past and the present.

Another example of how music can be held is through the beauty of the voice of international singer Andrea Bocelli. Listen to the richness of his gifts in *Canto Della Terra*. Andrea Bocelli is blind. His voice brings to my mind the words of Helen Keller, who accomplished greatness despite being deaf, blind, and mute. She said, "When one door of happiness closes, another opens; but often we

look so long at the closed door that we do not see the one which
has opened for us."

Often a child's voice needs to be opened up, having been closed
by emotional trauma. The song "Everybody Has Music Inside" is a
song that helps to accomplish this.

> Everybody has music inside, especially for you. Don't be
> afraid to let it out. It isn't hard to do. You don't have to be a
> virtuoso; it doesn't matter if you sing just so-so. It's a feeling
> down inside your soul so come on. You can do it! Everybody
> has music inside so let a song ring out. Just let it come right
> from your heart. That's what it's all about. Music is the sound
> of life reaching out for love. Everybody has music. Everybody
> has music. Everybody has music inside. (Greg & Steve 1980)

One of my private piano students gave me a coffee mug that had
printed on it: "A hundred years from now it will not matter what my
bank account was, the sort of house I lived in, or the kind of car I
drove, but the world may be different because I was important in the
life of a child" (Forest E. Witcraft, 1894–1967). On the recent New
York State writing tests for fourth graders, there was an essay question
asking about the person you look up to as a hero or heroine. One of
my learning-disabled students wrote the following, "She is the music
teacher here. I look up to Ms. Sobol. . . . She ask me to get on the
drums and she said I was good, after that I play and play and play."

See with your soul, hear with your heart, touch with the gifts
that you have each been given.

It Depends upon Y.O.U.
Presented at ABI/IBC Twenty-Seventh
International Millennium Congress on Arts and
Communications, Washington, D.C., July 5, 2000

Greetings and good morning everyone. You will recall that last summer in Lisbon, Portugal, my presentation was entitled "Communi-

cation through Music: A Language beyond Words," and my closing comments were for you to "See with your soul, hear with your heart, touch with the gifts that you have each been given." Today's message, which has developed from my daily experience with work with a diverse group of socially, emotionally, and psychologically learning-disabled students, is a message designed to raise your level of understanding about what is for many a hidden aspect of social consciousness. Through my work, I've seen that inside each and every child is a perfect human soul with unlimited potential locked up needing to be set free to find his or her ultimate power of expression. This message transcends all educational systems, and it transcends all cultures. For many of the special-needs and gifted children throughout the world, studying the creative cultural and musical arts process provides important breakthroughs in academic progress. More importantly, my work has shown me that it is not the child who suffers the disability but, metaphorically, it is us—it is our denial, discomfort, fear, intolerance, misinformation, pride, and prejudice. It is our blindness that hides truth and beauty. It is our ears that do not receive the processed message. It is our hands that need a guided strength.

Two recent current events demonstrated those attitudes that I live and teach. The first was the experience of hearing Bruce Springsteen singing to tens of thousands of people at Madison Square Garden his new ballad entitled "American Skin (41 Shots)." His was a voice of social conscience, the audience silently listening with respectful intensity. The troubadour used his position to make a statement to the masses about a very uncomfortable topic. The second experience was the Harvard University graduation address of Brooke Ellison. This young woman at age ten was hit by a car, paralyzing her from the neck down. No one expected her to live, but she has, dependent on two things—a respirator and the undivided care, support, and attention of her mother. Her message was one that I know well: none of us knows how life will unfold but miracles do happen. For these miracles one needs only to look at the people in your lives in order to see them.

I am extremely fortunate that I see miracles daily in my teaching job on Long Island, where I am privileged to instruct instrumental music to students ages five to ten, whose problems are so severe that they need alternate placement outside of their regular public schools. These children have shown me how much they can make a difference in the quality of lives of others. They are true messengers of life's wisdom. To start my audio-visual presentation, I have brought to you a performance of the Irish tenor Ronan Tynan singing a beautiful ballad by Phil Coulter entitled "Scorn Not His Simplicity." Mr. Tynan dedicates this song to those who are blessed to have a mentally or physically challenged child in their lives. As many of you are aware, Ronan Tynan was one of those children. Now we can all benefit by knowing about his life as a physician and singer. Following this video-clip you will see a select group of twenty-five children that I teach performing one of my original songs, "We Proudly Sing in Honor of Dr. King." This group of twenty-five wanted to participate in a countywide competition to show their understanding of the universal ideals of nonviolence, peace, brotherhood, and love that Dr. Martin Luther King Jr. dreamed of living. The lead singer is an eight-year-old with autism who demonstrates these truths to us. Next are fifty of my students who chose to participate in performances for Long Island's Very Special Arts Festival. This is one of the few opportunities these students have to mingle with the public in a community festival that features their abilities! The students represent a cross-section of the severe and multiple handicaps serviced by our partner in public education program. Rejoice with them as they sing "This Little Light of Mine."

Now it is your turn. It is one thing to recognize the message I am giving but it is another matter to put it into practice. We performed the musical play *How Does Your Garden Grow?* (J. Jacobson/J. Higgins, 1997, Hal Leonard Corp., all rights reserved) in March. Over two hundred special children were involved in the production. The photograph you see was a gift from my students. Each child singing in the photograph is considered intellectually challenged. They are dressed as garden vegetables and have important questions to ask you so that your garden of life can fully bloom.

Inside each and every child is a perfect human soul with unlimited potential locked up needing to be set free to find his or her ultimate power of expression, but it depends upon your own under-standing. It depends upon Y.O. U."

Chime [Big Ben melody]. Thank you for your attention and participation.

Joining in a Common Hymn
Presented at ABI/IBC Twenty-Eighth International Congress on Arts and Communications, St. John's College, Cambridge University, July 19, 2001

Good morning and welcome to the Music Room. There are three rules that we need to follow:

1. Sit in the designated seat.
2. Ask before you touch.
3. Try your best.

Any questions so far? Great.

It is with particular delight that I accepted the invitation to address our international delegation here at St. John's College. Since this is the third Congress I am addressing, this morning's presentation will be a continuation of speaking about my attitude and approach for teaching music to special learners and its universal applications for daily living. On Long Island, New York, my day-to-day teaching is with students ages five to ten who have severe social, emotional, psychological, and behavioral problems with learning disabilities. Their common cases show their lives shattered, oh too many times, at such a tender age. Through music, I can build for them a world that has wonder and beauty and that serves as a foundation for their education to strengthen their successful generalization of information in language arts, science, social studies, mathematics, movement education, and the creative cultural and performing arts.

In Lisbon, Portugal, at the twenty-sixth International Congress, my presentation was entitled, "Communication through Music: A

Language beyond Words." This presentation so inspired one of our delegates, Dr. Ulf Sunblad, that he wrote a poem to me, which he read during the question and answer session following the presentation. The poem was called "Universum." Its translation was printed in the June ABI Newsletter. [Show on overhead transparency original poem in Swedish by Dr. Ulf Sunblad, July 15, 1999].

UniVerse (One Song)
All world
Is united
In a common hymn,
Uni verse
Song of winds
Heard in
Trees and waters.
That's why
I love the world,
It sings
In air, in wood, everywhere
And all
Created beings
Know that tune.

Dr. Sunblad asked me to set this poem to music. With careful thought I have composed the music for this important text. It is sung by Swedish singer Lillemor Klang Zakkay. Let's listen [Play recording].

As educators, how can we reach certain disadvantaged or disabled children to make them responsible citizens in a global community? For me, the answer lies in teaching in a reality-based system, in a multisensory mode. Last summer in Washington, D.C., at the twenty-seventh International Congress, my presentation was entitled, "It Depends Upon Y.O.U." Y.O.U. is your own understanding that inside each and every child is a perfect human soul with unlimited potential locked up, needing to be set free to find his or her ultimate power of expression. To demonstrate, I'd like to share with you two key elements to my success for teaching music to special learners. One is in the use of the universal colors red, yellow, and green. The second is in the application of the universal shapes of circle, square, triangle, and rectangle.

[Show transparency of traffic signal.] Before you is a stop light. On the open road, red means "Stop," yellow means "Caution," and green means "Go." On the open seas, sound and light signals are used to communicate directions. All military personnel understand these signals for navigation. Applying this principle to the music room, the teacher can establish directions for classroom structure. Sound signals are based on the way we speak. Red is the "low" tone and green is the "high," or "Go," tone.

Examples: "Please stand up" = *low, low, high—red, red, green.*
"Please sit down" = *high, high, low—green, green, red.*

Adding our middle tone, yellow color, we say:

"Please get in line" = *high, high, middle, low—green, green, yellow, red.*

To bring closure to class, we say:

"Good job" = *high, low—green, red.*

Another classroom management technique is called "The Stoplight Exercise" authored by Daniel Goleman in his book *Emotional Intelligence.*

Red Light: 1. Stop, calm down, and think before you act.
Yellow Light: 2. Caution. Say the problem and how you feel. Set a positive goal. Think of lots of solutions. Think ahead to the consequences.
Green Light: 3. Go ahead and try the best plan.

It is remarkable that in nature these three colors are most prevalent. Let us look at a beautiful Lobster Claw Heliconia plant found in the rainforest in Peru [show overhead]. Here the bold red, yellow, and green coloring is to attract birds and insects for pollination. Its extreme opposite in nature is exemplified by the poison arrow frog—red symbolizes "stop" to its predators. "Stop, I am toxic!" Since our Congress is in England, it is interesting to note that the color scheme of red for "Stop" and green for "Go" originated in the British railway system; then it was adopted around the world.

Besides colors, we have shapes that can give our challenged youth foundations for lifelong learning. Underneath all of your chairs is a shape. Please join me in some fun while we play the Shape Game. (The game is taken from Greg & Steve, "We Live Together Series," Volume 3, Youngheart Records, 1987.)

Now let's go on the road again and look at the information signs for riders and drivers. Identifying now from a new perspective, you see that these signs are rectangles, squares, circles, and triangles that use red, green, and yellow signs, plus black on white for absolutely nonnegotiable facts. Each shape stands for a direction [show examples] and serves as a signal for cognitive understanding, acting as a guide for civilized behavior among people and nations.

This and more on my attitude and approach to teaching music to special learners is elaborated in my book of the same name, soon to be published. It is a compilation of experience gained through my years of teaching based on the belief in the unlimited potential for learning in all children.

When we listen to a song, the left brain basically attends to the words, the right brain attends to the melody, and the emotional center of our brain, or the limbic system, becomes engaged. Our musical intelligence activity involves our whole brain, and because of this phenomenon, one can link learning in every activity, culture, or continent to our other intelligences through music. Though the topography, geography, and languages may be different, what are consistent are the sounds of nature and man's expression of such. When we study how each creature, land or sea, sings its own song, we learn that this music can blend together in complete harmony.

I love my work, and it continues to show that there is an immortal spirit with full capacity to learn in each and every child, regardless of his or her disability. In 1841, Laura Bridgman, the first deaf and blind person to learn to communicate through language, proved this at the Perkins Institute for the Blind in Massachusetts.

Helen Keller followed, confirming this to future generations of the world. She wrote that "Optimism is the faith that leads us to achievement. Nothing can be done without hope and confidence."

And as I said before, and is worth repeating, "Great civilizations rise and fall, but we are all connected by the universe: Uni (one) verse (song)." Let us make a difference in the lives of the future children of the world. Let us join together in this common hymn, "Universum" [Play ending of "Universum"].

Thank you; it was *wonderful* speaking with you again this morning! Enjoy your day!

♪ FIVE ♪

CHAPTER

Pearls and Roses

From the Original Thoughts and Referenced Writings of Elise S. Sobol

There is no greater lively art than music for bringing out the learning potential of a student. —Music Success for Special Learners, *School Music News*, March 1995

♪♪♪

My most important function is to bring my students to a happy place in music where they feel safe, secure, and successful. —Communication through Music: A Language beyond Words. Lisbon, Portugal, July 1999

♪♪♪

Dealing with cognitive and affective functions, music provides language for communication and development of self-expression. —Music Success for Special Learners, *School Music News*, March 1995

Special learners can see a world of wonder challenging us to extend our own human potential. —Communication through Music: A Language beyond Words. Lisbon, Portugal, July 1999

Music is language beyond words. It is mathematics in process and progress. It is the science of sound and a study of history and cultures. It is architecture of form and geometry of design. Music is an essential part of healing, giving power to the will to succeed. — Music Success for Special Learners, *School Music New,* March 1995

The general music teacher has the inexhaustible resource for success with the use of the computer in the classroom. The love of learning is combined with the joy of music-making and the belief in the value of technology when the mouse is brought to the music room. —Music and the Mouse, *School Music News,* May/June 1995

This multisensory approach to music education and performance incorporates visual, auditory, and tactile feedback firmly rooting musical growth, building competence and confidence for the special learner. —Red, Green, Yellow Song, *NYSSMA Notes,* Vol. 1

In putting on an assembly program, each and every student must feel significantly important. The program must have an enduring learning purpose. —Assembly Programs, *NYSSMA Notes,* June 1995

The microphone and the video camera are indispensable teaching aids for the special learner. They help mold, instill a sense of pride and accomplishment, and help show musical talents not usually recognized. These tools are empowering for the education of the child with special needs. —The Magic Microphone and Awesome Video Camera, *NYSSMA Notes*, October 1995

We, as music educators, have the added capacity to feel and express our emotions directly and deeply. This is part of the creative gifts that we have been given and that set our discipline apart from others. Not only do we instruct the mind but we touch the heart. By caring, by directing, by disciplining, by showing how to be productive musicians we help our students with the tools of life. We plant seeds for self-esteem and determination for the special learner, so he or she can enjoy his or her life to its fullest. —It Depends on Y.O.U. (Your Own Understanding), *NYSSMA Notes*, February 1997

All students challenged, disturbed, or gifted need to express control of their own lives. When a student is responsible for making his own good life, he can feel satisfied and secure. Through music and the sounds of nature, we can assist in building up the shattered lives of our special students. Music education can profoundly affect the mental health and welfare of the students by teaching about peace, harmony, beauty, calm, silence, love, and laughter. —Loud, Louder, Loudest: Teaching the Dynamics of Life, *School Music News*, December 1998

See with your soul, hear with your heart, touch with the gifts that you have each been given. —Communication through Music: A Language beyond Words, Lisbon, Portugal, July 1999

In life, you must do that which you are most afraid to do. —ABI/IBC 26th International Congress on Arts and Communications, Lisbon, Portugal, July 1999

♪♪♪

Let the music be your angel wings to carry you through. —August 1999

♪♪♪

Inside each and every child is a perfect human soul with unlimited potential locked up needing to be set free to find his or her ultimate power of expression, but it depends upon your own understanding. It depends upon Y.O.U. —It Depends on Y.O.U. ABI/IBC 27th International Millennium Congress on Arts and Communications, Education and Culture Seminar, July 5, 2000

♪♪♪

For many of the special needs and gifted children throughout the world, the creative cultural and musical arts will provide this important breakthrough. —PTA and Cultural Arts at the Nassau BOCES Elementary Program Newsletter, February 2001

♪♪♪

Let these efforts serve as a reminder to all that the study of the cultural arts process, music in particular, is a key to lifelong optimism and the academic progress of our students. —PTA and Cultural Arts at the Nassau BOCES Elementary Program Newsletter, Feb. 2001

♪♪♪

For our students, this is the golden key for maturing into responsible citizens in a global community. —The Study of the Arts, Commentary, provided to Rochelle Casella, producer for a public television special on the arts, Rochester, New York, February 2001

Publications as Author and Contributing Author

Sobol, E. S. (August 1994). *Music Success for Special Learners, Inclusion Buzzword of Hope for the Future!* New York: New York State Council of Educational Associations.

Sobol, E. S. (September 1994). The Red, Green, Yellow, Song. *NYSSMA Notes.*

Sobol, E. S. (January, 1995). Assembly Programs. *NYSSMA Notes.*

Sobol, E. S. (March, 1995). Music Success for Special Learners. *The School Music News.*

Sobol, E. S. (May/June, 1995). Music and the Mouse. *NYSSMA Notes.*

Sobol, E. S. (November, 1995). Magic Microphone and Awesome Video Camera. *NYSSMA Notes.*

Sobol, E. S. (February, 1997). *It Depends on Y.O.U. NYSSMA Notes.*

Sobol, E. S. (December, 1998). Loud, Louder, Loudest. *The School Music News.*

Sobol, E. S. (October, 1999). Communication through Music: A Language beyond Words. *The School Music News.*

Sobol, E. S. (August, 2001). Is That Your Joanna There? The Musical Rhythmic Intelligence. How Fantastic! www.nyssma.org.

Sobol, E. S. (December 2001). Instructional Music Teaching for Special Learners. *The School Music News.*

Sobol, E. S. (2001). *An Attitude and Approach for Teaching Music to Special Learners.* Raleigh, NC: Pentland Press USA.

Sobol, E. S. (January, 2006). Battle Victorious with Music. *School Music News.*

Sobol, E. S. (March, 2006). Literacy Support: Applications of the Color Scheme Red, Yellow, and Green. *School Music News.*

Sobol, E. S. (July 6, 2006). Reaching Higher with Music in Special Education. ABI/IBC Inaugural World Forum, July 4–9, 2006, St. Catherine's College, Oxford University, Oxford, England.

As Contributing Author:

New York State Education Department. (2001). *Tools for Schools, Improving Student Achievement through the Arts.* Albany: The University of the State of New York.

NYSSMA and State Education Department. (2002). *Music: A Resource Guide for Standards-Based Instruction.* Albany: The University of the State of New York.

MENC. (2004). *Spotlight on Making Music with Special Learners.* Reston, VA: MENC: The National Association for Music Education.

Miceli, J. S., Sobol, E. S., Makowski, M., & Mergen, I. (Fall, 2006). "A Four Way Perspective on the Development and Importance of Music Learning Theory-Based PreK–16 Music Education Partnerships Involving Music for Special Learners." *Journal of Music Teacher Education* 16(1), 65.

New York City Department of Education. (2008). *Blueprint for Teaching and Learning in Music Grades PreK–12.* 2nd edition.

Films with Elise S. Sobol for Educational Television

C & M Communication & Business Management Consultant. (2006). *Reaching Higher at Emma School, Aruba.* Orangestad, Aruba: U.N.O.C.A. and Muchila Fundacion Creativo.

Maduro, Demetrio, Mackaay, Lila, Arends, Glenda. (July 1, 2006). Programa Nos Amigonan Special y Unico. Mihor cu nunca y exclusivamente na Kooyman. Aruba.

Conclusion

I T HAS BEEN a pleasure to update, revise, and add materials to this second edition for purposeful use by new and veteran teachers and administrators in public and higher education. Throughout the pages of this text, I have shown examples of an attitude and approach for teaching music to special learners developed with great joy and fulfillment for enhancing the social, emotional, psychological, physical, and intellectual well-being of every student. The strategies and methods can be applied universally to facilitate learning across the curriculum areas for our diverse school populations.

May the reader find this second edition text a helpful, inspirational resource and reference. With sincere gratitude, and best wishes,

> Elise S. Sobol
> Melville, Long Island
> New York
> July 2007

Landmark Dates and Updates in Special Education Law

PRIOR TO THE passage of Public Law 94-142 in 1975, children with identified disabilities were frequently isolated from their nondisabled peers, and others with certain hidden disabilities were categorized as slow learners when they had difficulty with reading, writing, spelling, or arithmetic. Local school officials had no legal obligation to provide educational access or supplementary services to children with disabilities, and many state laws permitted public schools to exclude children with disabilities.

The expansion of educational opportunities for children with disabilities is an extension of the civil rights movement.

- 1954: *Brown v. Board of Education of Topeka, Kansas,* is associated with ending racial segregation. It affected education of children with disabilities by establishing the right of all children to an equal opportunity to an education.

- 1970: *Diana v. State Board of Education, California,* established right of children with disabilities to public education.
- 1972: *Pennsylvania Association for Retarded Citizens v. Commonwealth of Pennsylvania* was an additional ruling.

Advances in teaching led to national interest in and appropriate education for children irrespective of disability.

- 1973: Section 504 of The Rehabilitation Act prohibits discrimination on the basis of a disability by the federal government and in federal programs and activities.
- 1975: Public Law 94-142, the Education of the Handicapped Act, was passed by Congress. Later renamed the Individuals with Disabilities Education Act (IDEA) in 1989–1990, it ensured a "free and appropriate public education" in the "least restrictive environment."
- 1978: The Gifted and Talented Children's Act, Section 902 Public Law 95-561 indicates that the terms *gifted* and *talented* identify youth with high performance capabilities across the disciplines and who may require special attention and teaching techniques.
- 1990: The Americans with Disabilities Act prohibits discrimination on the basis of disability. It includes private sector employment provisions for funds called Title I. Title I became effective for employers with twenty-five or more employees in 1992 and for employers of fifteen or more employees in 1994.
- 1997: Amendments made to IDEA to reauthorize and make improvements. This document is quite extensive and can be downloaded for specific clarifications. www.ed.gov.offices/ OSERS/policy/IDEA.
- 2002: No Child Left Behind Act (NCLB) is the new federal education law introduced by President George Bush and passed by Congress. NCLB has a major impact on performance of all schools nationwide. For details about implementation of this law in New York State, log on to www.nysut.org. Students with disabilities must have access to the same tests and Regents Exams as general education students. Only accommodations

specified on the student's individual education program or Section 504 accommodation plan may be provided.

- 2004: December reauthorization of Individuals with Disabilities Education Act (IDEA) signed by President George Bush—areas improved by American Federation of Teachers (AFT) on student discipline, employment standards for paraprofessionals, and paperwork burdens among other items (see www.aft .org/publications/american_teacher/February 2005).

  1. New legislation allows schools to remove students who "inflict serious bodily injury" to an alternate setting for up to forty-five days.

  2. New version of IDEA includes more flexibility for highly qualified veteran teachers to demonstrate their competence in multiple areas in special education without taking qualifying tests or requiring individual certifications.

  3. As of April 2005, this legislation is called the Individuals with Disabilities Education Improvement Act of 2004. The full document is available at nysut.org/research/bulletins/20050523idea.html.

Books for Young Readers Used in the Special Education General Music Classroom

THE BOOKS in this compilation have been used successfully by the author for music teaching and learning. They are generally available in bookstores and public libraries.

Adler, David A., illustrated by John Wallner and Alexandra Wallner. *A Picture Book of Louis Braille.* New York: Holiday House, 1998.
    Music students will delight in knowing that Louis Braille, who became blind at the age of four, loved music and learned to play the organ, violin, and cello. His development of the Braille system came out of his personal study of sonography, a code of raised dots designed for night writing by soldiers.

Archambault, John, and Bill Martin Jr., illustrated by Ted Rand. *Knots on a Counting Rope*. New York: Henry Holt and Company, 1997.

> A moving story of a Native American who was born blind and who had a special mission. Knots on a counting rope were used as a tactile means to keep track of things not seen.

Barasch, Lynne. *Knockin' on Wood: Starring Peg Leg Bates*. New York: Lee & Low Books, Inc., 2004.

> A winning story for every month, including Black History Month. Inspirational for building disability awareness and an educational tool for success in the performing arts.

Belafonte, Harry, and Lord Burgess, illustrated by Alex Ayliffe. *Island in the Sun*. New York: Puffin, 2001.

> The story features the popular performance of the song "Day-O!"
> A great whole-language story!

Belanger, Claude. *Literacy 2000: Poems, Rhymes, and Songs*. Sing-Together Books. Crystal Lake, IL: Rigby Education, 2000.

> Series includes:
> *The Circus*
> *The Caboose*
> *My Dog*
> *I Like the Rain*
> *I Was at the Zoo*
> *I Wear My Hat*
> *Talk to Me*
> *The T-Shirt Song.*
> A marvelous set of story songs for whole-language activities in the classroom.

Bock, Jerry, and Sheldon Harnick, illustrated by Ian Schoenherr. *Sunrise Sunset from Fiddler on the Roof*. New York: Harper Collins, 2005.

> A story to sing and read, enhancing literacy through music while teaching about traditions.

Brown, Margaret Wise, illustrated by Leonard Weisgard. *Red Light, Green Light*. New York: Scholastic Inc., 1994.

> A beautiful story and a great introduction to the concepts of red (stop) and green (go), which are used to teach foundations of

music harmony in the special education classroom. Low and high musical instruments can be used to put the story to sound.

Buscaglia, Leo. *The Fall of Freddie The Leaf: A Story of Life for All Ages*. Thorofare, NJ: Slack, 2002.

An allegorical constructive story by a renowned psychologist to teach children about life and death. Key words chosen for instrumental accompaniment enhance concept.

Celenza, Anna Harwell, illustrated by JoAnn E. Kitchel. *Pictures at an Exhibition*. Watertown, MA: Charlesbridge Publishing, 2003. (Includes CD recording of piano and orchestra versions of Modest Mussorgsky's *Pictures at an Exhibition*.)

A classic of the repertoire in a wonderful performance-literature presentation.

Campbell-Towell, Lee. *Cha Cha Cha Songs for Moving and Playing*. Milwaukee, WI: Hal Leonard Publishing, 1990.

Excellent selections for variety in special education music classrooms.

Clark, Dan, illustrated by Jerry Dillingham. *Puppies for Sale*. Atlanta, GA: Dalmatian Press, 1999.

An inspirational story by the author of *Chicken Soup for the Soul* books about a puppy with a missing hip socket and a boy with a leg brace. Its message is tremendous for positive character development.

Clément, Claude, illustrated by John Howe. *Musician from the Darkness*. New York: Little Brown, 1990.

A discovery story that goes along with the study of primitive society and the power of music delivered by a reed flute. A kick-off to many creative arts activities.

Connelly, Bernadine. (1997). *Follow the Drinking Gourd*, with music by Taj Mahal, narrated by Morgan Freeman. New York: Simon & Schuster.

A memorable story to teach about the Underground Railroad and the foundations of freedom in America. Designed for initiating a variety of classroom interests and activities.

Coveleskie, Sally, and Peter Goodrich, illustrated by Laura Friedman. *Henry the Steinway and the Piano Recital*. New York: Bright Sky Press, 2002.

A magnificently helpful story to ease anxiety in recital performance.

Crews, Donald. *Freight Train.* New York: Scholastic Inc., 1978.

A picture book that demonstrates slow and faster train movements. A perfect fit for a transportation music unit.

Curtis, Jamie Lee, illustrated by Laura Cornell. *I'm Gonna Like Me: Letting Off a Little Self-Esteem.* New York: Joanna Cotler Books, 2002.

A hilarious book that adolescents and young adults can use to develop a class music composition based on their own vocalizations. Develop the composition in ABA form for class unity. Very good for developing positive self-concepts.

Dillon, Leo, and Diane. *Rap a Tap Tap, Here's Bojangles—Think of That!* New York: Blue Sky Press, Scholastic, 2002.

A wonderful story of a famous performer. Use to enhance listening skills by playing instruments or body percussion to rhythm of rap a tap tap. Have gifted and talented students develop other tapping rhymes based on text of story.

Elder, Jennifer, illustrated by Marc Thomas. *Different Like Me: My Book of Autism Heroes.* London: Jessica Kingsley, 2006.

Great for collaborative programs between center-based special education and district-based classes. Opens the doors to understanding the unique qualities of every person.

Fifth-Grade Students, Temperance, Michigan. *Angel in Blue: Story of Ashley Martin.* New York: Scholastic, 2000.

A tribute by fifth-grade students to one of their classmates. A great help to students when a classmate becomes terminally ill. Triangles or delicate bells can be used for sound on key words like "angel." Sound builds student's ability to stay focused.

Forest, Heather, illustrated by Susan Gaber. *A Bakers Dozen: A Colonial American Tale.* Orlando, FL: Voyager Books, Harcourt Brace & Co., 1993.

A traditional story with moral retold with beautiful illustrations. Great for learning about colonial times during the winter holidays.

Fourth-Grade Students, Mabel, Minnesota. *A Band of Coyotes.* New York: Scholastic, 2002.

Math and music concepts with beautiful illustrations for classroom activities.

Garcia, Jerry, and David Grisman, illustrated by Bruce Whatley. *The Teddy Bears Picnic*, with audiotape. New York: Harper Collins, 1999.

A great way to hook your students to teach about safety in the woods and on a picnic!

Gatti, Anne. *The Magic Flute*, with CD. San Francisco, CA: Chronicle Books, Artworks Press, 1997.

From the classical repertoire—purposeful teaching with great appeal for students. Students can make their own magic flutes!

Gifted and Talented Students, University City, Missouri. *We Dream of a World*. New York: Scholastic, 2002.

Students can make up their own songs based on ideas in this book. Can be a day or a six-week curriculum unit.

Grieg, E. H. *Peer Gynt Fantasia Pictorial*. Adapted by Makoto Oishi, translated by Ann Brannen, illustrated by Yoshiharu Suzuki. Tokyo, Japan: Gakken Co. Ltd., 1971.

The story of Peer Gynt can trigger discussion about fact and fantasy as it applies to daily living. Music reading is enhanced by exciting melodies. Appropriate classroom performance and art activities can be developed from the story. Introduction about Edvard Grieg and his music!

Guthrie, Woody, and Pete Seeger, illustrated by Kathy Jakobsen. *This Land Is Your Land*. London: Little, Brown, 1998.

An American classic! Always has a place in chorus programs and classroom music units. Contains a "Tribute to Woody Guthrie" by Pete Seeger.

Hirschi, Ron. *A Time for Singing*. New York: Cobblehill Books, 1994.

A celebration of nature and all things that sing together in harmony. A useful book to talk about cooperation in the animal kingdom and its applications to humankind.

Hotchkiss, Gwen. *Music Smart: Ready-to-Use Listening Tapes & Activities for Teaching Music Appreciation*, with audiocassette. West Nyack, NY: Parker Publishing, 1990.

Varied music repertoire with worksheet applications that can be adapted to the special education classroom.

Howerton, Mari, and Karen "Maya" Sorensen. *Sing and Hum Bumblebee*. Raleigh, NC: Ivy House Publishing Group, 2005.
> Lovely illustrated book for pre-K/Kindergarten based on finding acceptance in life's situations.

Hubbard, Patricia, illustrated by G. Brian Karas. *My Crayons Talk*. New York: Henry Holt and Company, 1999.
> Rhythms, rhymes, and colors—a perfect book to use in developing musical literacy.

Hughes, Langston. *The Book of Rhythms*. New York: Oxford University Press, 1995.
> An exciting classic that shows sources of rhythm, the nature of rhythm, the rhythm of music, mysterious rhythms of nature, rhythms in daily life, and the vast concept of rhythm, which unites us all in time and space.

Joel, Billy, illustrated by Yvonne Gilbert. *Goodnight, My Angel, A Lullabye*, book and audio CD. New York: Scholastic, 2004.
> A contribution to literature by popular songwriter, used for special listening moments.

Judd, Naomi, illustrated by Suzanne Duranceau. *Love Can Build a Bridge*, with audiocassette. New York: HarperCollins Children's Books, 1999.
> A wonderful song with illustrated book for performance, used most successfully with special chorus for Valentine's Day performances at nursing homes and rehabilitation centers.

Keats, Ezra Jack. *Whistle for Willie*. New York: Scholastic, 1999.
> As a listening activity, have students play the kazoo or other preband wind instrument to develop better musculature on cue word "whistle." Book is an impetus for other story-telling activities.

Keenan, Sheila, illustrated by Ann Boyajian. *O, Say Can You See? America's Symbols, Landmarks, and Inspiring Words*. New York: Scholastic, 2004.
> History of our national anthem, "The Star Spangled Banner," for greater cognitive understanding and facility in teaching the anthem. Book includes information on celebrating American holidays including Martin Luther King Jr. Day, Presidents' Day,

Memorial Day, Flag Day, Independence Day, Labor Day, Columbus Day, Veterans Day, and Thanksgiving.

Lach, William, and Metropolitan Museum of Art. *Can You Hear It?* With musical CD, New York: Abrams Books for Young Readers, 2006.

> Great art to teach music repertoire combined to reach every student of all capabilities.

La Prise, Larry, Charles Macak, and Taft Baker, illustrated by Sheila Hamanaka. *The Hokey Pokey.* New York: Scholastic, 1997.

> It's fun, fun, fun and wonderful for speech/language and gross motor development.

Lennon, John, illustrated by Lynn Lancaster-Poh and Tilman Reitzle. *Imagine.* New York: Kensington Publishing, 1990.

> This beautifully illustrated version of the song helps students understand the genius of the songwriter and the magnitude of the message.

Lepscky, Ibi. *Albert Einstein.* New York: Barron's Educational Series, 1992.

> A biography of a one of our greatest minds of the twentieth century, who just happened to have learning disabilities and who was also, among his many achievements, an accomplished violinist.

Levine, Melvin D. *All Kinds of Minds: A Young Student's Book about Learning Abilities and Learning Disorders.* Cambridge, MA: Educators Publishing Service, 1992.

> This book is dedicated to the teacher caring for every child. Through the eyes of a young student, you will understand more about attention deficits, reading disorders, memory problems, language disorders, social skills problems, and motor skills problems. This is a masterwork!

Martin, Bill Jr., and John Archambalt, illustrated by Lois Ehlert. *Chicka Chicka Boom Boom.* New York: Simon & Schuster, 1991.

> Rhythm and rhymes—great for conceptual teaching!

Martin, Bill Jr., illustrated by Eric Carle. *Polar Bear, Polar Bear, What Do You Hear?* New York: Henry Holt and Company, 1992.

> Sound dramatization for class or grade, based on pages of this popular book.

Mattox, Cheryl Warren, illustrated by Varnette P. Honeywood. *Let's Get the Rhythm of the Band: A Child's Introduction to Music from African-American Culture with History and Song*. Nashville, TN: JTG, 1993.

> Useful throughout music inclusion programs.

McGovern, Ann, illustrated by Craig Phillips. *A Desert Beneath the Sea*. New York: Scholastic, 1991.

> Using the fascinating creatures of the sea as an example, students can learn about the variety in nature, including strange sand perch, tilefish, clownfish that change from female to male as need be, plus the symbiotic relationship of small goby and nearly blind bulldozer shrimp. This book is helpful in addressing sensitive discussions in middle and high school classes on gender issues and lifestyle choices. Use in consultation with guidance and counseling staff. Unexpected conversations sometimes result from learning about the lifestyles of music stars in the media. A great teaching tool at the right time.

Miller, Cristi Cary, and Jennifer Bennett. *A Tapestry of Tales: 8 Musical Stories from Around the World*. Milwaukee, WI: Hal Leonard, 2004.

> A lovely collection—useful to the creative music teacher.

Nelson, Kadir. *He's Got the Whole World in His Hands*. New York: Dial Books, 2005.

> Song literature that students can see, read, and perform!

Orgill, Roxane, illustrated by Leonard Jenkins. *If I Only Had a Horn: Young Louis Armstrong*. Boston: Houghton Mifflin, 1997.

> The Ambassador of Jazz had childhood beginnings in poverty. An inspiring story to empower students with social, emotional, and behavioral issues. The biographical profile coupled with his greatest hits provides endless curriculum material.

Perry, Sarah. *If*. Venice, CA: J. Paul Getty Museum / Children's Library Press, 1995.

> Illustrator shows extraordinary capabilities of the imagination, "If zebras had stars and stripes, if ugly were beautiful, . . . if music could be held."

Pinkney, Andrea Davus, illustrated by Brian Pinkney. *Duke Ellington*. New York: Hyperion Books, 1998.

Another inspiring story of a champion of challenges! Edward Kennedy "Duke" Ellington, a forerunner in the evolution of jazz, from Washington, DC, to Harlem's Cotton Club, to New York's Carnegie Hall. The book gives great sources, a videography, and song examples! Basic for every elementary music classroom! Supports jazz education and African American history units.

Prokofiev, Sergei, and Janet Schulman, illustrated by Peter Malone. *Peter and the Wolf*, with fully orchestrated CD. New York: Knopf Books for Young Readers, 2004.

Great classic with contemporary applications of learning about different caretakers. Why did Peter live with his Grandfather? Why was it important that he not go beyond the gates! Discussions of importance of following rules and staying within certain boundaries. Also discussion about protecting wolves. Identification and introduction of musical instruments always a favorite activity with this musical story. For instrumental ensembles a wonderful school production.

Raffi. Songs to Read: *Baby Beluga*. New York: Crown Publishers, 1992.

Raffi. Songs to Read: *Down By the Bay*. New York: Crown Publishers, 1999.

Raffi. Songs to Read: *Five Little Ducks*. New York: Crown Publishers, 1992.

Raffi. Songs to Read: *One Light, One Sun*. New York: Crown Publishers, 1990.

Raffi. Songs to Read: *Shake My Sillies Out*. New York: Crown Publishers, 1988.

Raffi. Songs to Read: *Spider on the Floor*. New York: Crown Publishers, 1996.

Raffi. Songs to Read: *Wheels on the Bus*. New York: Crown Publishers, 1990.

Popular songs of early childhood, made even more popular with accompanying books for students.

Rockwell, Norman. *Willie Was Different*. Stockbridge, MA: Berkshire House, 1994.

This is an awesome book to teach about the American artist Norman Rockwell and his personal feelings about being "different."

He uses the story of a starling to demonstrate how important it is for even an extraordinarily talented bird to remain in a nurturing, loving environment. Putting talents on display can be harmful to health and happiness! This is the only children's book written by Norman Rockwell.

Sabin, Francene, illustrated by Yoshi Miyake. *Mozart: Young Music Genius.* New York: Troll Communications, 1999.

A lovely presentation of the life of a child prodigy. A nice springboard to any number of Mozart favorites.

Seskin, Steve, and Allen Shamblin, illustrated by Glin Dibley. *Don't Laugh at Me*, with audio CD. Berkeley, CA: Tricycle Press, 2002.

Contains an afterword by Peter Yarrow of Peter, Paul, and Mary, endorsing the book and Operation Respect: Don't Laugh at Me programs for educators worldwide.

Seuss, Dr. (Theodor S. Geisel). *My Many Colored Days.* New York: Knopf Books for Young Readers, 1996.

This book is useful for developing sound compositions for elementary through college teaching. Students can work independently or in small groups. The colors and music form a strong foundation for teaching about great works of music literature.

Shriver, Maria, illustrated by Sandra Speidel. *What's Wrong with Timmy?* New York: Little, Brown Young Readers, 2001.

An introductory story about a child with disabilities and forming new friendships. It's very well done and can be used for inclusion enrichment in different educational and therapeutic settings.

Thompson, Mary. *Andy and His Yellow Frisbee.* Bethesda, MD: Woodbine House, 1996.

A terrific story about a boy with autism. It raises the reader's awareness of behaviors seen in the music classroom. A musical activity can be developed from the story for enjoyment of all students.

Trapani, Iza. *I'm a Little Teapot.* Watertown, MA: Charlesbridge Publishing, 1998.

Trapani, Iza. *Itsy Bitsy Spider.* Watertown, MA: Charlesbridge Publishing, 2004.

Trapani, Iza. *Oh Where, Oh Where Has My Little Dog Gone?* Watertown, MA. Charlesbridge Publishing, 1998.

Trapani, Iza. *Twinkle, Twinkle, Little Star.* Watertown, MA: Charlesbridge Publishing, 1997.

Popular songs put to illustrations for strengthening language and music literacy.

Waber, Bernard. *Courage.* New York: Houghton Mifflin Company, 2002.

Another book used for creative musical composition. Each student reflects on something that took courage to do and these concepts are put together in a class composition vocally and/or or instrumentally. Depending upon the level of the students, the composition can be notated and recorded based on each person's musical contribution. It is a very empowering activity.

Weeks, Sarah, illustrated by Lois Ehlert. *Crocodile Smile*, with CD. New York: HarperCollins, 1995.

Weeks, Sarah, illustrated by Suzanne Duranceau. *Follow the Moon*, with CD. New York HarperCollins, 1995.

Two wonderful volumes that combine science concepts with music. Both are extraordinarily interesting and useful at various educational levels.

Westcott, Nadine Bernard. *I've Been Working on the Railroad: An American Classic.* New York: Hyperion Books, 1996.

An American standard to teach about immigration and the building of the railroad, to include in a unit of American work songs, and a basic song with which to learn basic accompaniment chords on guitar or keyboard.

Wood, Jakki. *Fiddle-I-Fee: A Noisy Nursery Rhyme.* New York: Simon & Shuster Children's Publishing, 1994.

A traditional folksong that can be used in a variety of ways in the special education vocal and instrumental classroom or grade assembly.

Young, Ed. *Voices of the Heart.* New York: Scholastic, 1997.

A beautifully illustrated book with Chinese characters and visual collage that shows the variety of emotions found in our human heart. The virtuoso heart, the shameful heart, the understanding heart, the forgiving heart, the joyful heart, the sorrowful heart, the respectful heart, the rude heart, the contented heart, the aspiring heart, the frightened heart, the merciful heart, the tolerant heart, the angry heart, the evil heart, the silenced heart, the doubtful heart, and the loyal heart. An excellent book to use creatively along with the magical sounds of nature to build awareness of pleasant sound experiences in students with social and emotional difficulties. (See Sobol article that refers to *Voices of the Heart*, "Loud, Louder, Loudest: Teaching Dynamics of Life" in *Spotlight on Making Music with Special Learners*. Reston, VA: MENC, 2004.)

References

Web Sites

Americans with Disabilities Act—www.ada.gov/pub/ada/htm

Autism Society—www.autism-society.org

C.A.R.T.S. Culture Catalog—hkazama@citylore.org

Council for Learning Disabilities (CLD)—www.cldinternational.org

Learning Disabilities Association (LDA)—www.ldaamerica

Lighthouse Music School—www.lighthouse.org

National Information Center for Children and Youth with Disabilities (NICHCY)—www.nichcy.org

New York State Education Department Office of Vocational and Educational Services for Individuals with Disabilities—www.nysed.gov/vesid

New York State Union Teachers (NYSUT)—www.nysut.org

SMN: The New York State School Music NEWS New York: Westbury—www.nyssma.org

U.S. Department of Education Office of Special Education and Rehabilitative Services—www/ed.gov/about offices/list/osers/index.htm

U.S. Department of Justice—www.usdoj.gov

World in Tune—www.carousel-music.com/tune.html

References

Berkow, Robert, Mark Beers, and Andrew Fletcher, eds. (1997). *The Merck Manual of Medical Information Home Edition.* New York: Simon & Schuster.

Cline, Starr, and Diane Schwarz. (1999). *Diverse Populations of Gifted Children: Meeting Their Needs in the Regular Classroom and Beyond.* Upper Saddle River, New Jersey: Prentice Hall.

Gardner, Howard. (1982). *Art, Mind, and Brain: A Cognitive Approach to Creativity.* New York: Harper Collins.

Gardner, Howard. (1985). *Frames of Mind: The Theory of Multiple Intelligences.* New York: Harper Collins.

Glasser, William. (1982). *Stations of the Mind.* New York: Harper & Row.

Glasser, William. (1998). *Choice Theory: A New Psychology of Personal Freedom.* New York: HarperCollins.

Goleman, Daniel. (1995). *Emotional Intelligence.* New York: Bantam Books.

Greg and Steve. (1980). "Everybody Has Music Inside." From *We All Live Together*, Vol. 4. Acton, CA: Youngheart Records.

Dark, Ida D., et al., eds. (1996). *Music for All Children.* (Kit with facilitator manual, participant handbooks, and videorecording.) Washington, DC: VSA Educational Services and MENC.

KSE (Kids for Saving the Earth). "The Earth Is My Home." Plymouth, MN: Kids for Saving the Earth (www.kidsforsavingearth.org/index_high.html).

MENC. (1994). *National Standards for Music Education.* Retrieved from www.menc.org/publication/books/standards.html.

NYSED (New York State Education Department). (1996). *Learning Standards in the Arts.* Retrieved from www.emsc.nysed.gov/ciai/arts/pub/artlearn.pdf.

Perry, Sarah. (1995). *If.* Venice, CA: Children's Library Press.

Pierangelo, Roger, and Robert Jacoby. (1996). *Parent's Complete Special Education Guide.* West Nyack, NY: Center for Applied Research.

Rocha, Ruth, and Otavio Roth. (1995). *Universal Declaration of Human Rights: Adaptation for Children.* New York: United Nations Publications.

Skuy, Mervyn. (1996). *Mediated Learning in and out of the Classroom.* Arlington Heights, IL: Skylight Training and Publishing, Inc.

Sobol, Elise S. (1998). "Loud, Louder, Loudest—Teaching the Dynamics of Life," *The School Music News.* December.

U.S. Department of Justice. (2005). *A Guide to Disability Rights Laws.* Retrieved from www.usdoj.gov/crt/ada.

Young, Ed. (1997). *Voices of the Heart.* New York: Scholastic Press.

Index

About the Author

ELISE SOBOL, music educator and concert pianist, has been recognized for her unique contributions to the field of teaching music to special learners in noted biographical publications such as Marquis' *Who's Who in the World, Who's Who in American Education,* and the *International Directory of Distinguished Leadership.* Named to the 2005/06 National Honor Roll's Outstanding American Teachers, Elise Sobol has devoted a lifetime of service to education and has experience in teaching from early childhood through high school in regular and special education settings. A special education music teacher since 1988 for the Board of Cooperative Educational Services of Nassau County, she currently teaches students with autism and developmental disabilities at the Rosemary Kennedy School in Wantagh, Long Island. Ms. Sobol also teaches on the adjunct music education faculties of the New York University Steinhardt School of Education, Culture, and Human Development and the Long Island University/C.W. Post campus School of Visual and Performing Arts. She serves on the executive board of the New York State Council of Music Teacher Education Programs and since 1993 has been the Music for Special Learners Chair for the New York State School Music Association. Active as an international clinician, she has brought her interactive style of facilitative instruction to special populations in Europe, Asia, North and South America, Africa, and Australia, as well as New Zealand and the island of Aruba. As a pianist she has appeared in noted venues from New York City to Melbourne, Australia, as soloist, recitalist, and chamber musician. Elise Sobol is the recipient of distinguished awards including Long Island's Very Special Arts Award of Honor, citations from the New York State Assembly, nomination for New York State Senate "Women of Distinction" program, Ernest Kay International Foundation Award, among others. Ms. Sobol's educational background included specialized study in theory at the Juilliard School and piano with Murray Perahia at the Mannes College of Music with a Master of Arts degree in Music Education and Performance from Teachers College, Columbia University. Presently, Ms. Sobol continues with postgraduate studies in neuromusicology and special education to develop additional music teaching materials.

Praise for *An Attitude and Approach for Teaching Music to Special Learners*

"This book is for all music educators. It is both a philosophy and a 'how-to' book with a wealth of information. I believe it is essential for all educators and as such should be added to everyone's reference materials." —**Peter Brasch**, former president, New York State School Music Association

"[This] book helps teachers deal with special learners in the most positive and realistic manner, always respecting the child or individual for his or her attributes and abilities." —**Leslie Jones**, DMA, executive director of The Filomen M. D'Agostino Greenberg Music School at Lighthouse International, New York, New York

"I learned tremendously from the first edition, but I have learned even more in the revised and updated second edition." —**Ayumi Takeshima**, violinist, arts administrator, Crystal Arts, Inc., a Japanese management and consulting company for performing artists and musical events and performances

"[*An Attitude and Approach for Teaching Music to Special Learners*] is the most important new work being done in the field of music education." —**Petina Cole**, NARHA Certified Therapeutic Riding Instructor, Winslow Therapeutic Center, and vice president and COO, The Talking Pictures Company

"This is a book that must be read by every music teacher, whether a college music education major or a fifty-year teaching veteran. [*An Attitude and Approach for Teaching Music to Special Learners*] clearly defines the various definitions and types of disabilities, and it offers positive strategies for implementing new programs and concepts into the music classroom." —**Elaine Gates**, former president, New York State Council of Music Teacher Education Programs

"This book provides the reader with a solid baseline of how to teach children who learn differently. An invaluable resource book for all teachers of music." —**Patricia Cestaro**, The Music Health Connection

"A celebration for music educators, musicians, and general educators, this book is an elevator to music appreciation and comprehension of how much music can help children. I've never read a book that gives such a clear, useful approach for teachers as this one." —**Yehudit Carmon**, PhD, affiliated researcher of the School of Education, Bar-Ilan University, Israel

"This is such a comprehensive resource for teachers all over the world." —**Wendy Neilson**, professor in the Department of Human Development & Counseling, University of Waikato, New Zealand

"*An Attitude and Approach for Teaching Music to Special Learners* is a comprehensive and concise resource covering all aspects related to teaching special learners, including background information, general and specific pedagogy, and even very useful lesson plans and resources." —**Dr. Keith Kaiser**, chair of Music Education, Ithaca College